Surviving the Unwanted Divorce

Discover a Purpose-driven Life after the Devastation of Divorce

India L. Kern

ISBN 978-1-64299-822-1 (paperback)
ISBN 978-1-64299-823-8 (digital)

Christian Faith Publishing, Inc.
832 Park Avenue
Meadville, PA 16335
www.christianfaithpublishing.com

Printed in the United States of America

Dedication

Thank you to my sweet li'l birds, Nora and Ava Kern. God outdid Himself when He gave you to me.

Thank you to Bill Leversee, my soon-to-be husband and partner in life. I look forward to our future together. I appreciate your unwavering support regardless of how big my dreams become.

Thank you to my mother, who shaped me into the woman I am—quirks and all!

Thank you to my sister, Fran Slaughter. You're my earth angel who carried me when I didn't have the strength to do it myself.

Thank you, Jesus, for this life that I love.

I have been through the valley of weeping,
The valley of sorrow and pain;
But the God of all comfort was with me,
At hand to uphold and sustain.

—Mrs. Chas E. Cowman
Streams in the Desert

Contents

Preface 9

Introduction 11

    A Letter to You 13

    The Four Phases of Divorce 16

Part I: Entering the Valley 19

    My Story, Your Story, Our Story 21

    Taking the Death-Valley Bypass 24

    What's in a Walk? 27

    Finding Peace on the Leeward Side 33

    Sisters in Christ 37

    Exercise I 40

Part II: Settling In 41

    The Sweet Gift of Wisdom 45

    Creating the New Norm 48

    Walking the Circles of Grief 55

    Spectacular Dysfunction 58

    Exercise I 62

    Exercise II: Set your Core Values 63

    Exercise III: Counterbalancing the Cups of Life ... 64

Part III: Surrendering 65

    Psst . . . Your God-Sized Hole Is Showing ... 69

    The Apology 72

    How I Forgave My Ex 74

    Spiritually Bankrupt 79

    Thanksgiving Grace 83

    Exercise I: God Truths 86

    Exercise II: Finding God in the Valley 87

Part IV: The Gift...89
    Forcing Fruit..93
    A Moment of Sudden Revelation 98
    Walking through the Valley with Children in Tow 101
    Rules to Follow 102
    It's Going to Leave a Mark 105
    The Thank-You Note...109
Part V: Closing the Circle...111
    Life After Divorce 117
    Blooper Reel 122
Postscript..127
    What If?..129
    On the Fringe of the Valley 131

Preface

The book you hold in your hands came out of a marital cataclysm. At thirty-nine, without warning, I watched my husband walk out the door. With two kids, no job, and no backup plan, I was forced to stare down divorce, and all I wanted to do was to curl up into a tight ball and escape from my reality. In acute pain, I went into survival mode, but I had no guide to follow. Christian books did not relate to my situation, and mainstream books did not resonate with me. I wanted someone to show me the ropes. I needed a guide to walk alongside me in the valley, shepherding me through the stages from *married* to *divorced*. I never found the book I was looking for, so I decided to create it myself. My intention is for this book to guide you and all the others walking the same path through the valley of divorce.

Surviving the Unwanted Divorce is not only a book; it is my mission in life. In the middle of chaos, I found my purpose, and I want that for you too. If you would like to know how this book might impact you, take a look at the chapter "Life after Divorce" in "Part V: Closing the Circle." It will give you a glimpse into life's possibilities, and it shows how I walked in the valley and came out the other end.

Your story is in the making right now, but first, you must start. Start bleary-eyed and sleep-deprived. Start with fear. Start without understanding. Start with pain. Start with doubt. Just start the walk now.

Introduction

A good laugh and a full night's sleep can cure almost anything. When we add God to the mix, well, nothing is impossible. If you're not religious, don't let this book scare you. I consider myself more spiritual than religious, more godly than Christian. My relationship with God has grown as a result of divorce. Believing in something larger than myself and laughing along the way was how I survived the dark days. It has been, at times, a rough go. Not everything has turned out as I imagined. Mostly it has turned out better.

God said *no* to me. When I prayed to keep my marriage together, He denied me because He had something much better waiting. Writing this book has been a sacred walk to forgiveness, and the root of the book has been love. I didn't have this clarity until I was writing its final chapters. It's love for my ex-husband, and it's love for you and other women who share my same story. Pain can be the catalyst needed to set you free so you can embrace the future, making room for your full expansion and discovering the person God intended you to be.

Right now, we may be connected by pain, but by the end of this book, our connection will be through strength. This book will guide you on the walk from *married* to *divorced*. Not only will it show you how to survive the pain, but it will teach you how to find an overwhelming peace as you walk through the lowest points of the valley. Thank you for entrusting me to be your guide. I am honored to walk with you on this journey through the valley of the unwanted divorce.

A Letter to You

Dear friend,

You do not know me, but we share a similar story. I too dealt with a spouse that seemed to be a hologram of what I married. He greeted me at the airport with the simple words "It's over." Assuming he meant he was done with Southwest Airlines, I had no idea he was referring to our marriage. He dealt me a blow that became a wrecking ball to life as I knew it. My body felt as if I had been socked in the gut. This feeling stayed with me for weeks, *but* I am here to tell you it does not last.

At this moment, life may seem pretty dismal; that's probably why you picked up this book, but I promise you life will get better. You are walking through the lowest points of the valley, and there are three steps you must put into practice right now:

- Take care of yourself. Start with the basics: nourishment, sleep, and exercise.
- Lean on God. He is right there with you, and He has a hand in this, the good and the ugly.
- Rely not on your own understanding because, quite frankly, it makes no sense whatsoever. It may help to look at your spouse as being temporarily insane.

Clearly, we all do not have the same kind of ex or the same story, but there are some typical characteristics of men who jump ship with very little explanation.

I have discovered that a man of this nature will follow whatever satiates his selfish needs. He will make you the bad guy and even turn on you. He is full of anger and resentment. Shouldn't you be the mad and resentful one in this story? It makes absolutely no sense at all, but don't even try to understand it right now. Understanding will come later. He has lost his moral compass and seems nothing like the person you fell in love with. He will rewrite history, your history together. It's all an attempt to justify his actions.

Many times he cannot understand why you do not want him to be happy. Most likely, he has been thinking negatively toward you and the marriage for months. By the time he gets around to inform you, his decision has already been made. It's as if he expects you to know this telepathically. Usually, there is another person in the picture. This gives him the courage to make the swift exit out the door.

One thing I know for sure is, there was nothing I could have said to change his mind. I was forced to accept the breakup. I had no say in it, and it came as a *huge* surprise. Yes, we had marital issues like any couple of eleven years, but I didn't see divorce coming. It was a sucker punch to the gut, leaving behind a lingering stomachache for months.

What I have just described to you displays a massive life transition. A transition can be like a record scratch in life, causing an instant halt in the routine, catching you completely off guard. Transitions, as painful as they may be, are a part of the human experience. They require you to leave something behind in order to gain something new, and the *new* is significantly better than what you left behind—even though that may not seem plausible in the beginning of a transition. Knowing and understanding this simple concept will make divorce a little easier to swallow.

Before I tackle the details of a transition, I really want you to hear what I am about to tell you; no matter where you are right now in the divorce process, you *must* view this as an opportunity, a second chance, to create your best life *ever*. I'm living proof! I did it. Along this journey, I started out as a *victim*, immobilized by pain and trapped by the chains of my past. I cut loose, and I am free. It's time to break every chain that keeps you bound to a past that no longer exists, but first, you must invite God along the journey. There's no other way. And when you share your weakness with Him, He will give you strength.

I'm sure your story is not exactly like mine, but we share the same theme. You and I did not want a divorce, but we got one. The story goes like this: we married for life, but our partners did not. Now it's time for you to write your new story. With God as your coauthor, you can create this new chapter that can be better than you ever imagined. God makes beautiful things out of the muck and mire. He will take your mess and make it into your message. This will be your gift to the world, but in order to discover your God-given talent, you must first walk.

Even if all you see is darkness up ahead, unable to see any light through your struggle, God's light is within you. His light will be *the lamp to your feet and the light to your path* (Psalm 119:105). You may question the light inside; maybe it's only a flicker, or maybe it doesn't seem to exist at all, but it only takes a small flame to expel the darkness. If you have the desire to take the first step, Christ will show up for you. He will be the anesthetic to your suffering, and He will give you peace even in the abysmal pain.

God will never leave you or forsake you. Now having exited the valley, my life is richer in so many ways, emotionally, spiritually, and even physically. I worry less, and I sing more. I love deeper. I am forever changed. I think differently. I tolerate less. I know what I want and what I am supposed to be doing. I am on a clear path. I live with passion and purpose. I thank God for the walk through the valley. He had my hand the whole time.

Now I invite you to walk with me through the valley of divorce.

The Four Phases of Divorce

Every transition begins with an ending.
We have to let go of the old thing before we can pick
up the new-not just outwardly, but inwardly.
—William Bridges
Managing Transitions

An "ending" or "dissolution" is the definition of *divorce*; *divorce* epitomizes a transition. We all will go through transitions in life. That's one thing we cannot avoid, but transitions can serve as fertile ground for spiritual growth. That may be difficult to hear right now, but hopefully, after reading the pages in this book, it will make more sense. I have broken the book into five parts. *Parts I–IV* represent the four phases of a transition in a divorce setting, and *part V* is life after the transition. Once we understand what a transition entails, we then can determine where we are and what we can expect in the future.

The transition begins when you *enter the valley* or the crisis. In the *entry* phase, the disaster has hit, and you are left dazed and confused. You know you are in a transition when you feel anxious, restless, uncertain, isolated, and alone. You are still reeling, and you don't know which way is up.

Once you have realized this divorce thing is *for real*, then you move into an evaluation or *settling-in* period. I hunkered down in this space for a couple of years, trying to understand the whys of my situation. *Why did he leave? Why was I facing such heartache? Why me, God?* I rehearsed my past over and over again, analyzing the mistakes we had made as a couple. I never doubted I needed God through this tsunami storm, but I did question the motive behind so much pain. Times of understanding emerged when I was no longer sugarcoating dysfunction. I had to leave behind my old self so I could live a godly life.

I would swing from a point of examination to a point of understanding how God was shaping me. I hung out here for years vacillating between two points of *settling in* to my situation and *surrendering* to God's will. In the *surrender* phase, I started letting go of what no longer served me, releasing the need of control and the feelings of shame and failure. In this phase, you start to recognize the plans that God has in store for you, and you begin to align yourself with God's will versus your will, and a spiritual rekindling occurs.

Oftentimes, the *settling-in* and the *surrender* phases are times of feeling out of control or underwater. You mull over past decisions, and you become more open to change, maybe even adopting a new philosophy. Like an acrobat, you swing between surrendering and resisting. Don't be surprised if you hang out here for a while. You are still assessing your situation. There's more to learn, and you need to allow yourself plenty of time. As you lean in to God, you edge closer to understanding, revealing some clarity to the situation.

In the *surrender* phase, I knew a book was on the horizon, but I had to align myself with God's will in order for it to materialize. I knew I was on the right path, because it was the first time I felt at peace, at home, and I felt as if this was what I was made to do. I could not get enough writing in, always wanting to do more, many nights pulled away by dinner and the other duties I carried as a single mother.

As you recognize God's hand in all aspects of your life, you head into a directional phase called *"the gift,"* also known as the *"purpose and passion"* phase. It's the "aha" moment when you catch yourself saying "For this I was born." You have set your sails toward a point of destination, and you may not know how you are going to get there. When you are aligned with God, destiny experiences will occur to advance your passion and purpose, making it possible for you to see God's plan unfold. Toward the end of the transition, don't be surprised if you experience a faith challenge, where God pushes you to *practice what you preach.*

Writing this book has been my ultimate faith challenge, and the fact that you are reading this right now means opportunities showed up for me to publish my work and get this to you. Remember, the soil in the valley is fertile for your growth and expansion. Use this time to till the soil so the seeds planted by God will one day burst forth and reveal your fruit grown in the valley.

* Four phases and insights related to transitions come from the book, *"Stuck! Navigating Life and Leadership Transitions"* by Terry Walling. Used by permission.

Part I

Entering the Valley

My Story, Your Story, Our Story

Mountaintops are for views and inspiration
but fruit is grown in the valleys.
—Billy Graham

Shattered wide open, complete and utter devastation, crushed—this was my state of being as I stared down the face of divorce. Divorce was never the plan. It came out of nowhere, and I was left to pick up the pieces of my broken life. I felt like a failure. I had been a great mother, and I thought I had been an excellent wife. Life did not make a bit of sense. I was grasping at anything that would offer an explanation for my predicament.

I will never forget the cruel words shouted at me over the phone: "Get over it!" Those three words rattled me to the bone and ear-marked time. She was incensed and angry at me for still being hurt. It had been only a few weeks since my husband walked out the door.

How do I get over it? I couldn't see ever getting beyond this hollow misery because this was the collapse of life as I knew it.

I am a Southern girl from Macon, Georgia. It's a unique town that most people have only passed through while making a pit stop en route to the beaches of the Georgia/Florida coast. I met my ex-husband in fifth grade. I was interested in the new kid in the red parachute pants. I was young, so when I say "interested," I mean, I thought his pants were weird. He will tell you he noticed me too. We were only ten years old, but there was a definite magnetism between us. We were drawn to each other.

We later discovered that our mothers, acquaintances themselves, were pregnant with us at the same time, and we laughed about being "womb-mates." We became friends in sixth grade, and he gave me gum every day. As we matured, our friendship grew. He could make me laugh like no other person on this planet, and his humor was off the wall. Nothing was off-limits to joke about, and it never was. It felt very familiar because my family had an odd and unconventional way of laughing at our own dysfunction. We both used humor as a survival tool, wielding it with comfort and familiarity.

When we were in high school, we became even closer. He told me later he was always trying to get out of the dreaded "friend zone." In the adolescent years, he pined for me, and I did not feel the love until much later.

After I studied, partied, fell in love with an Italian, and ate my way through Italy, I came back to the States in 1995. I thought it was time to be an adult. He was there waiting. We started dating, and I started calling him Shooghah.

The name originated from a cat that we adopted. We named the cat Sugar, pronounced "shooghah" in the South. This cat was so hateful we had no choice but to change his name to Mr. Nasty, and then the pet name unexplainably transferred to my ex-husband (boyfriend then). We married, and two years later, we had our first daughter. The second daughter followed in 2005.

Signs of unrest started popping up two years later, and my life started unraveling. We regrouped and held it together for a few more years. Then 2011 hit, and my life, as I knew it, came completely undone. From that point forward, I was dealt blow after blow. When I look back, it all seems like an inconceivable story that I watched happen to someone else.

I picked up Shooghah from the airport after his trip to Vegas in May 2011. I knew things were shaky. He had left his wedding ring in the shower, but he promised it was an "accident." The night before, over the phone, we had an intense conversation, and he said that when he came back, he wanted to work on our marriage. I was genuinely excited about the prospect of restoring our relationship. The next day, I was blindsided.

At the airport, he opened the door, hurled his bag on the backseat, and coldly said, "It's over." That's it. That is how he ended the eleven-year marriage and the twenty-nine-year friendship. I had no choice in the matter. It was very clear there was nothing I could have said that would have ever changed his mind.

Little by little, the pieces started to fall into place. He had clearly moved on. He had a girlfriend with a baby on the way. Not only did I have to get used to his new life, but so did our little girls. Our speedy divorce was finalized, and his new life was just beginning. They married shortly after our divorce was finalized, *and* my therapist married them. Yes, you read it correctly. My *therapist* married them! Words cannot describe the level of betrayal I felt at this point in my life. It was as if I had been caught in a tsunami, and every time I came up for air, I got hit again with another wave, but somehow I continued to get sips of air. When I looked around me, all I could see were remnants left behind after the storm: the house we had renovated, family pictures on the wall, our dinner table, the art piece he gave me for my birthday, and even clothes in my closet. They all served as constant reminders of what no longer existed.

I was shattered wide open. I was one big gaping wound that could not stop bleeding. No one can understand this pain unless they have walked through it. I know there are other tragedies such as death that far outweigh divorce, but when you are the one left, you grieve like you have experienced death itself. This is awful to admit, but at the time, I thought I would have handled it better if he had actually died. Now with some healing behind me, I am happy my ex-spouse is alive and well so my children have a father to love.

There is no question that divorce is a death—the death of a marriage. If you share custody, you are faced with this death over and over again. Every time I dropped off the girls for their weekend with their father, I had to witness the new life he had hastily thrown together: new house, new wife, new kid, new life. There might as well have been a neon sign blaring the word "Rejected" every time I entered his driveway.

This was my real life, but it looked more like fiction. So as I was saying, his new life was beginning, but so was mine. I just didn't know it yet.

Taking the Death-Valley Bypass

When a person can't find a deep sense of meaning,
they distract themselves with pleasure.
—Viktor Frankl

Nobody wants to walk through the valley because, quite frankly, it stinks. *Isolated, confused, alone,* and *desperate* were just a few words to describe my state of mind as I stared at the road up ahead. Let's call it what it is—divorce is death valley. It's like walking through a hot, dry desert and you are thirsty for understanding. Nothing and nobody can quench this yearning. Not only is it the death of a marriage; it's the death of you as *wife*.

In this state, it's only natural to want to take the bypass and skip all the suffering. Unfortunately, there is no shortcut. You are in a furnace of pain, and the only way out is to go straight through. Avoiding the walk-through causes you to go on pathways that lengthen the trip. Diversions create unnecessary twists and turns along the journey and delay healing. New love interests; contrived busyness; self-indulgent behavior with food, alcohol, shopping, and sex are common distractions. Much like a drug, distractions numb the pain, but there's no sidestepping the discomfort. Sure, you can temporarily check out, but once the buzz wears off, you are left with *raw pain*.

It's crucial to implement self-control. If you stumble, believe me, God will give you ample opportunities to learn the lesson over and over again until you get it. You must understand—this is a one-woman journey. First, you must work on the vertical relationship between you and God to build strength and to find healing. You have to be comfortable in your singleness. If you rush the process, you will attract a reflection of yourself. And right now, if I had guess, you are not functioning at peak performance.

As a person who has traveled this path before, I want you to learn from my mistakes. I can save you the time, and you can learn the lesson without the hard knocks. I jumped in a new relationship way too early. It was my distraction of choice. I was raw, angry, broken, and depressed; I attracted a replica of myself. The new romance was my attempt to take that imaginary bypass around the pain. A new relationship may sound enticing, like a reprieve from reality, especially if you are the one left. Your ex-spouse may even already have a serious significant other, so why shouldn't you?

I discovered that rushing into another relationship only delayed my healing. The new love served as a diversion from my heartache. I felt unloved and discarded, and my self-esteem was flattened. I craved the attention he gave me, and it helped soften the dull ache left behind after being *disposed of*. It had been a long time since I had experienced such adoration. It filled the void of emptiness. I became wrapped up in a highly dysfunctional romance, and I hadn't yet cut the emotional strings to my ex-husband and the dysfunctional ties that kept us bound together. I was separated, not divorced, and I had no business getting involved with a new man, even if my husband had clearly moved on. I had been tossed out of the frying pan, and I landed in the fire, which became a continuation of dysfunction with no breaks in between.

The new relationship helped fill the emptiness and the loneliness. Instead of looking up to an infallible god, I was looking to an imperfect man to find comfort. My vision was limited to the horizontal perspective between a man and me, rather than the vertical perspective between myself and God.

I allowed my need to be with someone else compromise my core values. At the time, I had not established any core beliefs; naturally, I was meandering off trail. I was trudging along in the valley, but it was taking much longer to gain any ground. It also caused me to repeat history. It was as if I was stuck on a roundabout in the middle of the desert. Soon I discovered that the same things that bothered me in my marriage still bothered me in my new relationship, but I allowed the compromise. It was very clear I had attracted a clone of my broken self.

It was no surprise when the doomed relationship ended. I was back at square one, in death valley, alone, empty, and lost. I had taken some alternate routes off course, but the digression was not all in vain. I did learn what I did *not* want. It was a small but necessary step in the right direction.

When you enter the valley, you are in a vulnerable state, and you have a high chance of selecting poor partners. I like to blame it on what I call the postmarital fog that settles in right after the breakup and doesn't lift until there's evidence of healing.

In this state, you may choose a complete opposite of your ex, but don't be surprised if Mr. New Guy displays very similar negative traits of your former husband. It's just what we do until we know better. You must heal before dating. If this is your situation, I get it—no one wants to be lonely. I certainly didn't, and as a result, I learned the hard way.

But consider the alone time like logging hours on the flight of intense self-exploration. It's necessary to discover who you are and how you arrived here in the valley before you can truly give to another person. If you jump too soon, you jump into the fire, often-times finding yourself caught in a rerun of your past life.

What's in a Walk?

I have had a lot of worries in my life,
most of which never happened.
                                    —Mark Twain

Plain and simple, the valley is a scary place to be, but in order to take life by the horns, you have to leave something behind. Let's start with the past. Stop staring in the rearview mirror. Glances are allowed, but don't fix your gaze on the rear. Instead, briefly reflect at the past as something to learn from, not a place to hang out in. Never set up camp in the valley; instead, be a visitor just passing through.

I witnessed a friend who just entered the valley. Her divorce was not like my breakup, quite the contrary. She'd been counting down the days for her *soon-to-be* ex to leave the house. It took them awhile to actually physically separate. As a bystander, it was like watching someone pull off a Band-Aid, one hair at a time. Some of us, like myself, had the fortune of getting the Band-Aid ripped off with one quick yank. Yes, I said "fortune" because I was lucky. There was no dillydallying about whether the divorce should happen or not. It just did. Granted, I did not have much say in the matter, but my point is, it was a blessing.

I did not waste years trying to figure out my situation. Instead, I got hit upside the head. It hurt, but after a while, the wound healed. I like to think the wound is where the light of the Holy Spirit entered. Rumi, the thirteenth-century Persian poet, said this quote first, but he left out the bit about the Holy Spirit, and that, to me, is the most critical piece to the puzzle.

Divorce is just that, where you find yourself staring down a ten-thousand-piece puzzle dismantled in a heaping pile in front of you. You know you are going to have to put it back together again and some pieces are missing. You must place piece by piece back in order, one step at a time.

Oftentimes, fear takes over, and when you look at the circumstances in front of you, the future looks bleak. It may even bring you to a standstill. This is when you have to choose between fear and faith, between control and surrender. Fear says, "Stop! Do not go forward." Trust says, "Walk!" Growth requires taking risks, and risks involves fear—supersized fear. So here you are at the edge of the valley. You have fear coursing through your body as you stare at the walk ahead. Fear can easily overrule trust.

In fact, the opposite of fear is not courage; the opposite is faith, believing in something that you cannot see. Fear translates to avoidance, regret, stagnation, and a halt in personal growth. Fear keeps you rooted in darkness and stuck in pain.

Fear has many facets. It can cause paralysis when it comes to decision-making. Sometimes it's a lot easier to stay grounded in your story, rather than having to create a new one. When you are scared of change, you set your gaze on the past and pitch a tent in the valley.

In my experience, *setting up camp* translated to me taking on the victim role, and I got a lot of attention from it. I also blamed my ex-husband for my unhappiness, but the truth is, no other person has that kind of power over me. I had to stop assigning my ex-husband to be the *peddler* of my happiness. I learned I had an amazing ability to be happy, and it was dependent on my relationship with Christ.

Your ex-spouse does not complete you, and no other person ever will. You are complete with Christ—period. When you invite God into the valley, you are placing Him as first in charge and relying on Him to make order out of the chaos; this is what He does best! This means taking God at His word, walking in His obedience, and believing that you can and will do all things through Christ.

You may not understand why you are in the thick of pain, and it's okay to question it. Naturally, we doubt; that's what we do as humans. Rick Warren says, "It's part of having faith." And there's no better way to learn of faith except through life's trials.

To walk by faith seemed out of reach for me until I realized its true meaning. When I was at the bottom, in the depths of pain, I reached out to God and begged for help. There were many unanswered questions as to why my husband was leaving me. I remember standing in the shower crying, already physically exhausted from the day's worth of sobbing, and speaking out loud to God, "I know you will make good out of this. There's a reason for all this hurt, and you will show me the lesson one day, then I will have peace."

I had faith even in the darkest hour. Although I didn't understand why my husband had *discarded me* in such a callous way, I knew God had a plan and, one day, He would reveal it to me. It was *trusting in advance for what will only make sense in reverse* (Philip Yancey).

In the wounded state, I was vulnerable, and I had to be careful. It's a dangerous place to be. Either faith or fear gets the upper hand, and for me, it changed on a daily basis. It required believing what God promised was true. The evil twins of worry and self-pity, many times, kept me stuck in the pit. A successful day was living in the boundaries of a twelve-hour day when faith and gratitude prevailed.

When we play out the *what-ifs*, we are experiencing unnecessary suffering. Think about it; a crisis should only be experienced one time, when it actually occurs, not rehearsed over and over again in the mind. Don't be the person who reflects on her life and realizes so much suffering was endured by events that never actually happened.

If you look at your outside circumstances alone, you are walking by sight, not by faith. Sometimes *what appears to be* and *what actually is* are drastically different situations. Look at social media for example. Most people post a better version of themselves, even if their lives are in the crapper. I'm sure you know a few. They convey a false message. It says, "*Look, world, my life is perfect*," versus their true reality—just proving, you cannot go by sight alone.

Now apply this to your life. What *appears to be* is not always true. You must rely on God within you to provide comfort. Nothing and nobody can create it for you, making happiness an inside job.

Each day may bring new trials, but it's just one more step closer to completing that colossal puzzle. This is a journey of reliance on Him. Many times I found myself thinking I was in complete control. "I got this, God" was an attitude that launched me into self-destructive patterns. Thoughts of self-doubt and worry were my *go-to* sentiments. Sure, I had been dealt an impressive wallop, and as a result, I obsessively worried for the first two years after my divorce. I was really good at it. If it had been an Olympic sport, I would have taken gold. Worry happens when fear trumps faith.

Funny thing is, worry never changed a thing; it just showed how little I trusted God. Imagine you are drowning in the ocean and, when God comes in for the rescue, your flailing arms and panic-stricken movements interfere with His help—when all you really need to do is just throw your hands up and say, "God, I know you got this, because I certainly do not." It's the act of relinquishing control, and many times, it's no small feat to accomplish.

During one of my epic bouts of worry and self-doubt, I had a conversation with my mother. At that time, I was building Faithful Warrior, my Christian yoga business. I was giving free classes for the exposure and to help our church community. It seemed like Faithful Warrior would never take off. As I was complaining about my lack of success, Mom showed me how my idea of success was off target. She pointed out that the worldly view of success was based on the outward display of money, and it wasn't based on how a person walks through life. How you conduct your life determines your success. It has nothing to do with money. God doesn't judge success by how much we make, what car we drive, or what house we live in.

She made me realize I was a success because I was a child of God; that was enough. Financially speaking, Faithful Warrior was in the hole, but spiritually, it was a triumph.

It was uncanny how my yoga was attracting women who needed healing, many from a broken marriage. Initially, they connected to me based on our common pain, but little by little, a transformation was taking place. They were getting stronger, and so was I. It was the perfect symbiosis between teacher and student. They were teaching me as much as I was teaching them.

But here's the kicker: if my apple cart had not been overturned, I would not have had the life wisdom I do now. Wisdom is the light in the dark, and once the bulb is turned on, darkness cannot compete. Now that I have light, I will not go back to fumbling my way through the darkness. God's light has illuminated my path so I will not lose my way.

When I was struggling, stuck in fear, and dodging the act of forgiveness, I had a special dream. I believe God was speaking to me in attempt to bring peace and forgiveness to my heart.

In the dream, I vented my anger and frustration on my ex-husband. I unloaded everything I was upset about. All the muck that entangled me on a daily basis for the past two years of my life came to the surface. In the dream, he listened to everything without judgment. I was finally heard, and there was no rebuttal. My ex-husband was fully present, and this act of listening was healing to me. Even though it didn't happen in reality, the dream itself was a gift.

In the dream, it was as if God downloaded a year's worth of therapy sessions. I woke up lighter and more aware of my past than ever before. It was enlightening, and it occurred to me that people come into our lives to help us work out our core pain. If we do not get it the first time around, God puts it back in our face to deal with again.

In my marriage, we did a dance with each other to bring healing around some deep core wounds. We both brought *hurt* to the table that needed to be healed. What I discovered from the dream changed my entire philosophy and belief system around my painful past.

I discovered that for years, I had been grieving for an absent father who was stricken by alcoholism. The ending of my marriage acted as a trigger that launched me into the same core pain I experienced as a child. I needed to finally feel the grief of my childhood. So instead of regretting the past, I now know my divorce served as a tool to find forgiveness and healing for a father and for an ex-husband. I no longer have one foot stuck in the past of resentment and the other stuck in the future of fear. I can be fully present in the now, which is the ticket to contentment.

I cannot force you to choose trust over fear, but I can tell you that when fear dominates, it changes our life from an outlook of abundance to a perspective of scarcity. When you limit your focus to what is wrong in your life, you are taking Jesus out of the equation. He did say, "*I am always with you.*" Why do we have so much trouble believing Him?

Have you ever considered what God wants to reveal to you through this hardship? Start by asking yourself, How is God shaping me through this divorce? How do I see God's hand in the walk through the valley? I know the beginning of the walk is brutal, and it's difficult to see any good in the pain. A successful day is mustering up more trust than fear. It's walking by faith, not by sight.

You must simply *trust more*! You will never regret trusting in the Lord. God will give you God-sized support to counter the Herculean challenge, but He insists you continue to walk forward. When fear gets the best of you, you are setting up camp in the valley when you were only meant to pass through it.

Approach each obstacle day by day, hour by hour, even minute by minute if necessary. It's easy to get caught in the setbacks of the past and the *what-ifs* of the future. Let those go. One has already happened, and the future one may never even materialize. Your focus is on the now, because this moment right now is the only one you can actually do something about.

Finding Peace on the Leeward Side

A smooth sea never made a skilled sailor.
—English Proverb

Have you ever noticed that many times the people who have had the most difficult lives oftentimes are the most peaceful and gentle individuals to know? These people are like experienced sailors who have weathered the storms of life. They will not crack under pressure, and you want them around you when a crisis hits.

I once heard a true story from a local pastor in my hometown of Macon, Georgia. His experience one night at sea has stuck with me over the years and has been the ultimate illustration of trust in the midst of a storm.

An experienced sea captain invited the pastor on a mission to meet a Norwegian freighter thirty miles out to sea off the Georgia coast. Pastor Turrentine accepted the invitation. Late at night, on a cabin cruiser, they started the journey heading straight into a storm. The rough conditions didn't faze the sea captain as he pushed through the oversize swells. Their task was to meet the freighter then pilot the massive ship through the canals and channels, which were foreign territory to the Norwegians.

Waves crashed over the bow of the cabin cruiser as it forged ahead. It was being tossed around like a cork in the ocean, bobbing up and down in the giant waves. The trip was long, and the pastor was very aware of the total blackness that surrounded the boat. After spotting the distant lights of the freighter, the pastor questioned the captain on how he planned to board the ship in such rough waters. The skilled seaman calmly responded, "Just wait and see."

They drew closer to the ship to see the twenty-five-ton Norwegian freighter majestically positioned like a mountain in the ocean, hardly being swayed by the tempestuous waves. The two captains exchanged light signals, and then the pastor witnessed something quite spectacular.

The enormous ship started to turn sideways, blocking the small boat from the giant waves and gusty winds. The waters calmed, and the captain of the cruiser nestled his boat alongside the huge vessel. On the ship's leeward side, the ocean was now a lake.

Then the captain climbed a ladder with ease to board the freighter so he could pilot the ship through the Georgia channels.

Isn't this exactly how our relationship with Christ should look like? Like the immense freighter, God's massive love will protect us in life's storms. God is the leeward side, and He will offer refuge, but you must lean in, nestle alongside Him, and be confident you are going to get past this predicament.

Sometimes God calms the storm, and other times, He calms the person caught in the storm. My divorce was the squall of my life, and it happened as quickly as a divorce can go down.

In May 2011, my ex left. Six months later, the divorce was final. One month after that, he had a baby with his girlfriend, whom he married right away. It was all happening so fast, and it was difficult for me to digest. I was in shock as I witnessed my ex-husband build a new family in a matter of months after leaving ours. It seemed everywhere I turned, I had to meet the discomfort head-on.

One day, I was running errands, and I looked up to see a larger-than-life poster of my ex's new wife plastered on the window across the street from my pharmacy. It was around seven feet tall, filling the entire storefront window. It was an advertisement for the gym they opened together, but it felt like a display of their fresh start, a renovation to the old, stale past life with me. I stared looking at the revealing poster, crushed by the weight of my feelings of rejection, inadequacy, and betrayal—betrayal, because this was my territory, my pharmacy, my village and that used to be my husband. How dare my ex be so unsympathetic and indifferent to my feelings.

I get it; I had no business claiming dibs on the entire town, but I was crushed by grief, pressed to my edge, and I was mad as hell. I'm not a big fan of cursing, but that day, I was. Everywhere I turned, I was confronted by my singleness—the new life I wanted no part of. It was in my face, taunting me with the question "Where's your new life?"

I was already building my life, step-by-step, even though it seemed, at that moment, like I was standing still. Each step I made, I shed a little fragment of the blinders that kept me attached to my previous life with my ex. I was surviving. I was raw, vulnerable, caught in the vice grips of grief. It didn't seem like God was on my side. It seemed as if I was being punished and isolated. Where was my advocate in this? Where was God?

I was like the cabin cruiser caught by surprise in the middle of a violent storm. Almost sinking as I plunged deeper into the waters of pain, I somehow always popped up, cresting the next wave, the next challenge. God was there. He was making me face the naked truth head-on, over and over again. He showed me what my life really looked like. I don't mean my divorced life. I mean, He made me question who I was and what I stood for. He pressed me to my limit, but I didn't sink. I could not put any slant on the situation to beautify it. It was ugly, and it was not normal.

God removed me because I couldn't do it for myself. I was loyal to my marriage, almost to the point of suffocation. Determined to make my marriage work, I convinced myself I was fine, but I was living a life with no substance, brimming with denial. God was my advocate, and He did me a favor by pushing me off the edge and nudging me to walk through the valley. I had no choice but to leave my old life behind to learn how to be me. It was a "holy kick in the pants." As time passed, the blinders fell off completely. I could see for the first time. I was not living the life God had intended for me.

I had to find God on the leeward side, lean in, and nestle beside Him, letting Him take on my storm. He didn't calm the storm, and it raged on, but His gigantic love gave me refuge. It's now time for you to do the same. Your storm doesn't have to define you.

You will one day be the weathered and skilled sailor. Your character will be tested and strengthened because of the storm. In no way is it comfortable. In crisis, we squirm; we resist. It's what we do as humans, but there's a takeaway. When your eyes are open and you finally see, no longer blind to the truth, you will align your life with God, and a life lesson will follow, but your first assignment is to wait, lean in, and listen for God's cues.

* Story taken from the Macon *Telegraph*, "There's Safety of God's Leeward Side" by Pastor Reese Turrentine.

Sisters in Christ

So in Christ we, though many, form one body,
and each member belongs to all the others.
—Romans 12:5 NIV

Two years into my divorce, I visited a furniture store to check out a couch for a friend. It was a high-end, modern French store where you admire the low-cushioned white couches and bright-colored enamel dressers but wonder how in the heck anyone keeps it clean with a house full of sticky small hands.

It was the place I used to frequent with my ex-husband, and as a married couple, we had their signature couch, the one that resembled a red Shar-Pei, and it collected our girls' graham crackers and goldfish crumbs in each of its folds. From my own experience, I quickly learned that you most certainly cannot keep a high-end couch clean if you have kids and live a normal life. (Ironically, now I have a low white couch, but that's a long story and a very bad decision.) Strangely enough, I don't know what happened to that red Shar-Pei couch, and I haven't even thought about it until now as I tell you my story.

Upon entering the store, which happened to be in the neighborhood of my ex-husband's new gym, the sophisticated saleswoman approached me, admiring my fake Burberry scarf. The saleswoman introduced herself and then asked my name. I told her, and she paused then looked at me with a peculiar expression. She cocked her head to the side, in the direction of the gym with the full frontal window exhibition, and through her body language, I could tell the wheels were spinning as she tried to figure out my place in the story.

She recognized my last name, and then suddenly, she brought her hands to her face, almost covering her eyes, and said in a French accent, "Non, are you the ex-wife?" Cupping her hands around her face, she said, "Oh my god, you are so beautiful." And tears pooled in her eyes. Not only was I flattered, but instantly, I understood this stranger knew my story, and I had not said a word, except my name.

We plopped down on one of the brightly colored low couches, and we both noticed she was wearing a sideways cross bracelet just like mine, and immediately, there was camaraderie. This meant we were sisters in Christ.

She started telling me how I was better off and all the things that you don't want to hear when your husband has left but that end up being true. I never saw her again, but that day, the lady with the accent at the fancy French furniture store impressed me.

We were joined together by pain. I would think, at her age, she probably had seen her fair share of marital breakdowns. If it wasn't hers, maybe it was her daughter's or a close friend's. I wish she knew how very special that day was for me. Many days, I had felt invisible, like no one cared, but this stranger cried for me, for my pain. That's because she was my sister, related to me by the body of Christ.

I suffered, and she suffered with me. She was coming alongside me with support and living out the kingdom of God, because the kingdom was inside her. She listened when prompted to speak to me. Her empathy strengthened me. I felt like I belonged to a club of sorts, a fellowship where she knew my story, my pain. I instinctively knew she too had seen its depths.

Just feeling this changed something inside me. It made me feel better about humanity in general. Maybe society had a moral compass after all and my brutal dissolution did, in fact, have an effect on others even if it did resemble a Telemundo soap opera.

Like this woman, I am in your pain as you walk through the valley, and one day, you will be in someone else's pain. This will be your opportunity to come alongside a person and genuinely say, "I know how it hurts, and you will get through this." And you, my friend, will get through this too because you are a part of the body of Christ and we all work together. This is the meaning of *church*—not a place, but a family to belong to.

Look, we all are going to have to climb steep mountains at some point in our lives, but you have the choice to climb this mountain with your hands wide open, knowing you will never be abandoned by God the Father. Once you embrace this concept, you become *unshakable and assured and deeply at peace* ("The Message," John 16:32–33), even smiling in the middle of the storm.

Exercise I

List the distractions keeping you from advancing forward.

Where in your life are you overindulging? In what areas can you apply self-control?

What is in your rearview mirror that keeps you stuck in the past?

List the fears you face when you think of the future.

Give examples of how God has shown up in the valley with you.

Part II

Settling In

The *settling-in* phase was coming to the realization that the divorce was happening whether I liked it or not. It was a time of reflection, rehearsing past events with different scenarios, thinking maybe if I had made different decisions, it would have saved our marriage. In this difficult time of contemplation, I felt as if I were drowning, grabbing at anything that would make sense of my situation and keep me afloat. Unable to change my situation, I was forced to change myself, and by doing so, I was rewarded many times over.

The Sweet Gift of Wisdom

*You cannot be lonely if you like the person
you are alone with.*
—Wayne Dyer

I remember the first weekend my kids went to stay with their dad. The pain was excruciating. I was a stay-at-home mom. That was my title. In a matter of weeks, my identity seemed to be stripped from me. In fact, I didn't know who I was, what I stood for, my value system, or even how to be alone. Worst of all, I did not enjoy being by myself.

The unwanted solitude was a gift that contributed to my growth and healing. I needed alone time to really grasp how I arrived in the valley in the first place. In the quiet space, I rekindled a relationship with God. I didn't need any distractions to take away from the study of India. Although it seemed I was alone, God's presence was with me. It was in the stillness where I gained wisdom. I learned it is not true *loneliness* if you enjoy the person you are, and I was starting to love the person I was becoming.

I was *settling in* this space. I knew I was here to stay and there was no *undoing* my divorce, which was soon to be finalized. But it was in this space of stillness and quiet where breakthroughs were made. I realized I had an extremely high tolerance for dysfunction. For the first time, I could see how I played a hand in the disintegration of my marriage. My father, the severe alcoholic who was absent from my childhood, taught me how to pick a partner. His characteristics as a father and a husband, as flawed as they were, were all I had ever known. Even though the man I married had his shortcomings, he was never as bad as my dad. My father had set the dysfunction bar high, so mild dysfunction went undetected.

I could see I was choosing partners that reflected characteristics of my dad. With lots of therapy and a hearty appetite to recover, I dived into all types of books. Reading was my refuge. It helped me unravel the mystery behind my gravitational pull to dysfunctional relationships, rather than healthy ones. One of my favorite therapists shared with me the wise words "We all are just waiting on the bus that takes us back home." I jumped on that bus quite a few times before I could identify the problem. It took effort to truly see dysfunction for what it was, to not accept it as something I could fix, and to make no compromises while seeking a life with purpose.

In order to move beyond my past and find purpose, I had to identify my responsibility in the fall of the marriage. Even if my husband had left me, I still played a part in the divorce. It takes two to build up a marriage and two to tear it down.

Being newly separated, this concept was too abstract for my mind to grasp, and at first, I claimed zero responsibility. After all, he was the one who left, not me. If it had been up to me, I would have stuck it out. And that right there was part of my responsibility, or "irresponsibility," that led to our divorce. I accepted things that were unacceptable, which created a *standard* that we came to live by. My needs were not being met, and I am sure he felt the same. It boiled down to me not giving him respect, and he withheld love from me. We were caught in a vicious cycle. Our lack of awareness and incapacity to stop the loop of dysfunction cultivated a toxic space between us. Much like a riptide, the waters appeared calm on the surface. We looked like an ideal couple, but underneath the outward appearance, there were underlying currents of resentment. Eventually that's what took the ship down.

We did a poor job of what the Bible instructs husbands and wives to do: "Wives, respect your husbands. Husbands, love your wives" (Ephesians 5:33). Love between a married couple demands wives to actively and persistently respect their husbands, and husbands must actively and persistently love their wives, and we ignored that fundamental principle. I never would have had this insight without the "unwanted" solitude. It gave me the sweet gift of wisdom where I gleaned lessons from my past, rekindled a relationship with God, and strived for a life with purpose.

Creating the New Norm

When we are no longer able to change the situation,
we are challenged to change ourselves.
—Viktor Frankl

A habit cannot be tossed out the window; it must
be coaxed down the stairs a step at a time.
—Mark Twain

I f a habit takes time to *undo*, then creating a new one is that much more difficult because it demands that an action be taken. Unmistakably, divorce is an energy-draining machine, so finding the stamina to take action seems about as likely as you performing some type of miracle here on earth.

It's finding yourself deep in the trenches, surviving each day. You're tired, spent, and thirsty for information that would explain why this is all happening. You carry a backpack of shame that weighs you down, but it's time to dump it. You do not have to carry this burden any longer. Now is the time to apply gentleness to your life.

Gentleness means loving yourself so much that you make your spiritual, physical, and emotional health a top priority. It's nurturing yourself by cultivating daily practices of devotion, prayer, journaling, and exercise. It's believing that your body is a temple of the Holy Spirit and honoring it in such a way. It's relinquishing old habits that are not working for you and creating new ones that will strengthen you. It's *going within* so you will not *go without*. At first, the quiet may be uncomfortable, or you may grow restless. There are so many other things that can easily pull your attention away.

The laundry can wait, and so can the dishes. This is so much bigger than housework.

I resented the *unwanted solitude,* but I learned that stillness was the very thing that brought insight to my life, and it ended up being the primary tool to my recovery. I had been out of balance, my spiritual life was lacking, and all other areas of my life were deficient as a result. I needed stillness for my peace of mind, health, and overall well-being.

I discovered *being still* was not a waste of time; it was when I heard the voice of God. It was the grand pause, the quiet calm where my focus turned from myself to God. Remember, God gave us the simple instruction—"Be still, and know that I am God" (Psalm 46:10). There is a reason it was written, because so much repair can be done in the stillness and quiet.

The stillness was a time to reboot my system; it was a much-needed rest for the soul where breakthroughs were made. It was the crucial step needed for me to deepen my connection with God and to develop a better understanding of myself. I had to make an effort to turn down the racket of the world to hear God's gentle whisper. And then, I was finally able to see my dysfunctional life for the first time.

Some say it takes twenty-one days of practice to form a habit, and others say the magic number is 66. Either way, the point is, you must create the habit of scheduling time for God at least twenty-one days straight in a row for it to stick.

Also, the daily practices of meditating, praying, and journaling were critical in my spiritual growth and gave me stamina when life felt like an uphill battle. When I wrote, I gave voice to the pain. My journal became the keeper of my sorrow, relieving me from the backbreaking weight of so much hurt. As I dumped the shame and burden on the pages, I was mending my broken heart.

Equally as important as stillness and journaling, exercise was a fundamental tool that boosted my mental state and kept me physically healthy. I walked, ran, surfed, and I taught Christian yoga. All these activities served as a form of meditation. I left the cell phone at home, and I was forced to deal with the uncomfortable space of my thoughts. In the midst of physical exertion, I learned how to harness my anxious mind chatter while honoring the holy temple God had given me.

Not only did I want to be physically fit; I needed to keep my stress levels low to stay healthy from the inside out. I could see how stress wreaked havoc on my body. Once I became aware of its result, I could manage it or avoid stress altogether. Keeping myself healthy also meant nourishing my body with wholesome food, being careful not to overindulge, and getting plenty of sleep to recharge my body. These small but essential choices displayed the act of applying gentleness to my life by setting up new rituals and habits that nurtured my body, mind, and soul. In essence, I was creating a new norm for myself.

There were three areas of my life that I had to constantly take care of and pay attention to. They were my physical health, my spiritual life, and my emotional well-being. Understanding the maintenance of your physical health and spiritual life is relatively straightforward, but your emotional well-being requires *awareness*. *Awareness* is abstract and difficult to teach. If I were to ask you "How is your emotional state of mind?" and your answer is simply "I'm unhappy," you need to dig deeper.

How did you arrive here in the valley, in the unwanted divorce? Questions like this require *awareness*, and it requires deep self-reflection, through therapy, reading and research, even listening to the point of views of healthy friends and family. In no way do I want to undermine your feelings. You certainly have the right to express your *unhappiness*, but look at the root of your divorce. Question why you chose the partner that you did. There's a level of accountability that must be taken in order to achieve self-awareness.

Some people never reach a point of awareness, and then there are others who are just too darn scared to dredge up the dormant emotions that have been lying low for years—because once the emotions come up, they have to be dealt with, and that's the frightening part.

If you are struggling with fully understanding the meaning of *awareness* or your state of emotional well-being, accept the fact that, *we do not reach clarity alone* (Terry Walling, *Stuck! Navigating Life and Leadership Transitions*). We need people to process our experience with us. They can give us the insight that we are not cognizant of. Find a therapist, a coach, a mentor, or a levelheaded friend. The right question can trigger a new way to view your situation, giving you the gift of awareness and accountability, allowing healing to take place.

After identifying the three key domains of my life—physical health, spiritual life, and emotional well-being—I discovered I had to *counterbalance* all of them before I could realistically give energy to others.

I use the word *counterbalance* instead of *balance* because balance is impossible to achieve. Gary Keller and Jay Papasan, in their book, *The One Thing*, go as far as saying "Balance is a lie," but to *counterbalance* is attainable. They give the example of a ballerina *en pointe*. The ballerina appears to be the epitome of balance, even weightless; in reality, her toe shoes are vibrating, and she is making small adjustments throughout out her body to create the perfect *counterbalance*.

If your physical health, spiritual life, and emotional well-being are cups, how are you filling each one? Where are you lacking?

Ask yourself, What's the one thing I can do to improve my physical health? What's the one thing I can do to improve my relationship with God? And what's the one thing I can do to improve my emotional well-being? (Questions inspired by the book *The One Thing* by Gary Keller and Jay Papasan.)

Counterbalance means filling all the cups, maybe at different times, maybe at different levels, but being sure not to neglect one cup for too long. On some days, the physical health will be less than the emotional well-being. Maybe stress has been getting to you and you have been overindulging, but you had a coaching session and now have more clarity on your situation. Or maybe, on Sunday, you heard a profound sermon that filled your spiritual cup, but you didn't put any energy toward the other two areas. As long as you are giving toward all three cups, even if it's at different intervals and in different amounts, counterbalancing will happen. And when you start giving toward all three areas, you will see other parts of your life enhanced, such as your key relationships and work.

I intentionally left the areas of family (key relationships) and work out of the mix for now, because you must concentrate on getting yourself healthy before you can give to others. Clearly, if you have children, your life doesn't stop so that you can focus solely on yourself, but be aware of how much and how often you are concentrating on the three major cups. Once you are capable of counterbalancing, then you will see you have more bandwidth to contribute to the other key areas of your life.

All these areas overlap and intersect, so when one is completely neglected, you can expect to feel a deficiency in the other areas. Counterbalancing can be tricky, but it's doable, and it gives meaning to the idea of applying gentleness to your life. Consider it filling your tank so then you can give to others.

There was a time in my life when my cups were completely empty. My spiritual life was dry; my emotional state was unstable. I was lonely, and I didn't know why. My physical health was crumbling. It was late in my marriage, and I was getting hives all over my body. I never knew what I was going to wake up with. Sometimes, if they were on my face, I couldn't leave the house. My lips would swell three times their normal size. I looked like a victim of domestic violence or a casualty of an inexperienced plastic surgeon. As you can imagine, this unpredictability was frustrating. I was tested for every allergy imaginable, and I was not allergic to a thing, except my situation—or as my mother says, I was allergic to my marriage. In fact, I used to jokingly say this book was going to be titled *My Husband*

Gave Me Hives, but I decided bitterness and petulance are not a good look for anyone.

My body had been alerting me for years, and I was not listening. Or maybe I had been denying any thoughts that pointed toward the truth. The hives and other random health issues came up while I was still married and kept on for years after the divorce.

During my marriage in 2010, I received a doctor's call after a routine mammogram. The mammogram found calcification in my right breast. It was a scare, and the doctor said it was something to watch closely.

Five years later, I went back for an extremely overdue mammogram. The doctor was amazed. There was absolutely no sign of calcification. Both the doctor and technician were in awe, and they asked, "What did you do differently?"

I said, "I got a divorce!"

There was a cancer in my marriage that was growing. It was destructive to my health, and I believe if we had stayed together, the 2015 mammogram results would have been grave news. The malignancy of the marriage manifested itself throughout my body. Even though cognitively, I denied my negative situation, my body's internal system was flashing DANGER. The hives were my body's physical warning signs alerting me to fix the problem.

The problem was my marriage, and it was broken. I was accepting the unacceptable. I remember one Christmas Eve when the kids and I were the only sober people in the house, surrounded by stoned family members. It was sad, and I knew deep within my being it was not how I wanted to celebrate the birth of Christ.

Drugs made an appearance in my marriage all too often. I can define years of my marriage by what drug my husband favored. Two thousand ten was the year of marijuana. His office was like a free dispensary, and many *friends* traipsed through its doors. The year of weed was much easier than the year of Adderall. On Adderall, I watched my husband transform into a skinny smoker full of rage, and then at night, he used Ambien to downshift into a comatose state of sleep. Even testosterone and human growth hormone crippled our marriage. Whatever drug it was, they all drove a wedge between us.

Many people argue with me about the addictive nature of certain drugs. Whether it's addictive or not, if taking the drug is damaging to the person, to his way of life, and to those around him, then it's a problem. The crazy thing is, I knew this type of dysfunction or *addiction* all too well. I had been raised in it, but when it came to my relationship, I kept peace, and there was a price. As a result, my body took on the stress. I compromised everything from my health to my value system.

Divorce forced me to look in the mirror and reevaluate what I stood for. It involved deep introspection with a heavy dose of awareness. It was an opportunity to create a new life with no compromises.

You may be at the point where you want to heal but don't know where to begin. Like a pilot, you have to set a point of destination in order to arrive at your desired location. Your core values must be defined, and this will serve as a road map to your future. Here are my nonnegotiables. At the end of the chapter, there will be an exercise for you to define your core belief system too.

India's core beliefs:

God is my center. He is my savior and protector.

Family and Home are my sanctuary.

Honesty (integrity) is a trait I highly value of myself and expect from others.

Love and respect are necessary in my marriage and family relationships.

Service is the most important expression of faith.

Walking the Circles of Grief

*I will not let anyone walk through my mind
with dirty feet.*

—Gandhi

Time is the enemy as well as your friend in the walk through the valley. At least, that is the way it seems. In the beginning, from one minute to the next was excruciating to get through. I remember wishing I could teleport into the future to avoid the misery of the day. This was very contradictory to the image of the *fully present* yogi I presented to the outside world. Time is slow in the healing process, but time is necessary to heal. Patience is a mighty force needed on the walk-through, and you may ask, *Why is God doing this to me?*

My response to this question is, *Why not you?* We all suffer at some point in our lives. No one is immune to pain. In fact, if anything, suffering is the equalizer. It doesn't discriminate. It just makes you belong that much more.

Have you ever thought maybe this was the plan all along? We tend to view life as a collection of random events with no meaning. People who view the world this way are putting limitations on God's work. As a Christian, *you know that everything fits in a pattern for good to those who love God* (Romans 8:28). When you find yourself down in the dumps, fretting over the strains that divorce brings, imagine God whispering to you, "This is my doing."

My marital nosedive was necessary to awaken my deaf ear. I was oblivious to how far-off I had veered from God. After the crash and burn, the blistering pain was God's way of shouting to me, "Come back! You're off course! Follow me!"

God's plans are so much bigger than we could ever imagine. You are here for a reason; it's not by accident, and the suffering is not in vain. God uses the trials to teach you. The divorce is your tutor, and now is a good time to learn. There are some key ingredients you should know about time and how to get through the *day-to-day*, especially if you are new to the valley.

1. *Patience is a necessity.* God does not work to fit your schedule. David G. Allen said, "Patience is the calm acceptance that things can happen in a different order than the one you have in mind." You did not marry with the intent to divorce. The fact is, you are here now, and you must move forward. Rather than focusing on the "why me?" bit, let's discuss a plan of action.

2. *Grief is a key process you must go through.* You will walk through five stages of grief: denial, anger, bargaining, depression, and acceptance. Know you will not tread through these stages in a linear fashion or necessarily in that order. Instead, imagine you are walking circles around each stage of grief, sinking into it, really feeling it. When you are done processing a stage, you stop circling the emotion and move forward, but don't be surprised if you revisit a grief emotion after you thought you were done with it.

3. *Be the observer in the process, rather than the judge.* Do not put a time frame on each stage. When you approach grief as the observer, you are less likely to scrutinize your feelings, and you are more likely to see the purpose in the pain. With this come positive coping skills like forgiveness, compassion, and hope. Be open to pain. I know that sounds like a bad inspirational quote, but seriously, I am telling you to be open to *feel* the pain. Step into your pain, but lean in to God. You have to move through it, but you don't have to do it by yourself. He is with you always.

Feel it, sink deep, grieve it, and move on! Do not stuff feelings inside. Cry out loud. Let the emotions fly, and know that walking the grief circles is necessary for healing. When you go to a dark place, just look at it as being one step closer to moving beyond the pain.

Spectacular Dysfunction

In order to love who you are, you cannot hate
the experience that shaped you.

—Andréa Dykstra

When you are walking on the sidewalk and something trips you, usually your first reaction is to look back to see what caused the stumble. When you slip in life, you do the same, because our past can tell us a lot about our present-day selves.

I looked back at my past to understand where it all went wrong. Questions filled my brain, and when I started to examine my childhood, it gave me insight as to why I made the decisions I did. Digging deep into my past, I could see how comedy was my family's coping mechanism. It lightened the severity of the volatile situation at home. Laughing was the equivalent of lifting the lid off a pressure cooker, where we could release tension and escape the heated circumstance for the moment. As a result of my *stranger-than-fiction* childhood, my family found humor in the dysfunction. Laughter became the antidote to the stress caused by the chaos at home.

Surprisingly, I'm not ashamed of my family's dysfunction; neither should you, because it's what links us humans together. *Dysfunction* is not exactly a happy subject, but sometimes it offers priceless comedic fodder, and it seems my family had no shortage of it.

In 1979, my sister and I were sitting in our orange Volkswagen bus, impatiently waiting for my mother to finish cleaning the entire house before we went to the beach for a weekend getaway. It seemed our house was only clean when we left on vacation. Even as a child, it boggled my mind why my mother broke her back cleaning our massive house before we left on a trip. I understood not wanting to come back to a dirty house, but when the norm was mind-blowing disorder, I didn't understand why she felt the need to clean when no one was there. Well, my dad was there . . . kind of, at least to sleep. A tidy house would certainly go unnoticed by him, especially after a hard night of drinking, his nightly ritual.

My sister Jorie and I were growing weary of waiting for my mother. Jorie had just received her driver's license. She had the van running and was chomping at the bit to drive. In a rush, she jumped out of the bus to badger Mom one last time.

Our Southern colonial house sat at the top of a hill where the driveway curved around to meet a very busy street called Pierce Avenue. There was an embankment off to the side of the house that displayed red camellias in the spring. After waiting alone in the bus, I decided to try my hand at convincing Mom to stop cleaning. I was all of seventy pounds, and when I jumped out, that was just enough movement to start the ball—or in this case, the van—rolling. And since Jorie did not put the parking break on, the orange van started its descent. The passenger door was open, so I put my hands against the door in attempt to stop the moving van, but quickly realized I had nothing on this large machine. I stepped to the side and watched the big orange bus roll off the embankment, bumping down the hill and coming to a violent halt as a tree caught the passenger door, almost severing it from its frame.

I was in awe. *Did I do this? What if I had stayed? Would I have been taken on the jarring ride backward down the hill?* Worst of all, this meant we were not going to the beach anymore.

When my mother saw the wreckage wedged between the camellia bushes and the trees, she was horrified but more scared of what was to come after my father saw the damage. I then watched my mother immediately go into "solution mode," jump-roping the door shut and duct-taping plastic to create a window. To my utter delight, this meant we were still going to the beach. The makeshift window was a bit noisy and drafty on the four-hour drive, but it did not stop us from singing the whole way to our haven, the ocean.

The ocean has always been our family's refuge where we could enjoy the day just *being*, where there were no worries of what was to come. The therapeutic mixture of salt and sand scoured away the concerns carried over from 445 Pierce Avenue, our home that was heavy-laden with my father's alcoholism. My home was not a place where I could invite friends over, because then they would know the truth. Once they entered the beautiful house, they would no longer believe we lived a normal life; instead they would witness spectacular dysfunction that lay just past the threshold of the front door.

My house was a filmset facade, beautiful and stately. Little did people know, it was barely propped up and could come crashing down at any moment, leaving our family exposed for what we truly were: *liars*. We lived a life that seemed so normal, and yet we made midnight runs to my grandmother's house to flee my dad's wrath.

Like most alcoholics, my dad chose to air his contempt at night. And in the morning, I still went to my private school as if nothing happened. We hid behind my mother's Southern charm, fitting in at sport events and even debutante soirées. My mother was strikingly beautiful and always charming. She did the best she knew how. We got by.

Aware that I had inherited my father's genes, I knew there was a slight chance I too may experience a hint of insanity. It didn't help that my mother reinforced this thought. In my early teens, she would drag me to Alateen, warning me that if I did not attend, I was bound to go crazy. I haven't gone crazy yet . . . I guess, I still could.

The optimist in me believes, as a result of my warped childhood, I am more in tune with my fellow man. There's nothing unique about my story. That is the equalizer of suffering. It does not discriminate. It just makes you belong that much more. As twisted as it may sound, I am grateful for the dysfunction. It made me wiser.

In case you are wondering whatever happened after the bus incident, it was not as bad as you would think. In an effort to conceal the mangled bus, my mother parked on the right side of the garage, placing the passenger side millimeters from the wall. After arriving home from work, my father found the parking situation to be odd and investigated it more thoroughly. He discovered the makeshift repair and lit into my mother. Maybe it was a short rant on her incapacities as a driver, but it must not have been too bad, because all we remember is the unencumbered fun we had that weekend at the beach.

There's beauty in tragedy, and I thank God for giving me the eyes to see it this way. It is not natural to approach a crisis with eagerness or glee, but what if we moved toward each new crisis with the question, *what opportunities will this bring?* How different would our lives be? The crisis then takes on a new meaning. Maybe instead of wearing the shameful title of *divorced* or *child of an alcoholic*, you wear it like a badge of honor. You claim it! I am here having survived the crisis, so I can help others who follow behind me on the walk through the valley, and I will use my experience to come alongside them in their pain and offer support on the journey I have already traveled. What a difference it makes when you know there's purpose to your pain.

VW Bus Circa 1979

Exercise I

What responsibility can you claim in the divorce? Even if *divorce* was not your choice, list a few things that contributed to its collapse.

Exercise II: Set your Core Values

Think about the "non-negotiables" in your life. What is it that you will not budge on? Once you set your core foundation, it will serve as life's road map.

———————————————————————————→

———————————————————————————→

———————————————————————————→

———————————————————————————→

———————————————————————————→

———————————————————————————→

———————————————————————————→

Exercise III:
Counterbalancing the Cups of Life

Pick *one* thing that you can do to improve your physical health, spiritual life, and emotional well-being.

1.

2.

3.

How did you arrive here in the valley of the unwanted divorce? (Remember, *awareness* is necessary to answer this question. If you don't know the answer, seek guidance from a friend, mentor, or coach.)

*Book your free thirty-minute consultation with India L. Kern, a divorce recovery mentor, at www.indiakern.com.

Part III

Surrendering

As I started to accept that I was, in fact, a divorcée, I was inching out of the *settling-in* period of evaluation into a period of *surrendering* to the will of God. Like a pendulum, I swung back and forth between these two states. I would have successful days of aligning myself with what I thought God intended for me, and then I would quickly regress into thinking how I could have done things differently to avoid the divorce, even though I was fully aware divorce was here to stay. I was ricocheting between moments of clarity and periods of confusion, typical emotions of a transition. It was a time of mulling over, contemplating my circumstance, and coming to terms with where God wanted to lead me. As I look back, it was evident I was healing, even if I did fluctuate between acceptance and surrender for a couple of years. The notion of being *healed* is somewhat of an obscurity; we may get over the hardship, but we still carry the scar. It's the place that no longer hurts us anymore, but tough skin is left behind. It's a mark of past hurt and should serve as a reminder to never repeat.

As I swung between the phases of *settling in* and *surrendering*, I could not wait to be happy again, but I didn't quite understand the meaning of *happiness*. We all have a definition in our minds, but just maybe, our idea of happiness is not God's intent for us. Maybe it needs to be revamped.

Many times, what we want and what we need are two very different story lines. I think about what I was praying for in the beginning of this walk, and I thank God for not answering my prayers back then. I thought happiness was keeping my marriage together, plodding along, mending what I could with temporary fixes, but God knew best. He had a different plan altogether. Thank goodness, He did. I love the battle-scarred India a whole heck of a lot better than the unblemished girl from the pre-divorce days. I was forever changed. After the knockdown, I started to see my life for the first time for what it really was. I recognized my denial of how things seemed versus how they really were, but it required my life to be completely dismantled to see the striking imbalance.

Psst . . . Your God-Sized Hole Is Showing

*Getting over a painful experience is much
like crossing monkey bars. You have to let go at
some point in order to move forward.*
—C. S. Lewis

I was raised in a Southern Baptist church. We attended most every service that was offered, morning and evening, midweek and weekends. On Sundays, we attended Sunday school, and then the main service followed. I called it big church, because it was clearly only for the adults. Inevitably, one of our stomachs would grumble, I think, out of protest to the never-ending sermon. The pastor's way of preaching was in the form of yelling, and it seemed we, the congregation, were always in trouble. I didn't fully understand what my mother got out of these services, because it seemed like work to stay awake. A highlight of the hour was listening to my mother sing the hymns when her voice strained to reach a high note she had no business attempting. If my sister and I caught each other's eye, we spent the rest of the service trying to stifle our snickering. And when my nephew came, the chances of being escorted out of the sanctuary ran pretty high. We were not bad children; we were just bored children.

In college, I decided not to attend the Baptist church anymore. Instead, I chose the Catholic religion. Well, *chose* is a strong word. I was living in a small hill town in Cortona, Italy, so there wasn't much of a choice in the matter. Here I was, an American who did not speak Italian attending a Catholic church. Truth be told, I had trouble understanding Catholic services in English, much less in Italian.

My late twenties and early thirties could be summed up as a spiritual drought. Sure, I was a believer, and I even considered myself a Christian, but my actions didn't reflect my beliefs. I needed to clean up my act a bit. Simply put, God was absent in my life. Obviously, He was there, but I was not open to receive Him. Many times I was sad, and I felt empty. I didn't know why, but I had an inkling. Now I know why. I had moved too far from Christ, and I had a hole where God should have been. Although I had a religious foundation, I had no idea how to have a personal relationship with Christ. I was in a spiritual dry spell.

Then I married a non-Christian, which didn't help my spiritual development. He never discouraged me to practice my faith, but Christ was not a part of our household. The few and far-between occasions when I went to church, I went alone with two small children in tow.

I wish someone had pulled me aside and whispered, "Psst . . . your God-sized hole is showing." I don't know if I would have actually listened, but I believe it would have made me question the meaning behind the comment. The idea of a gaping hole where something is missing is unsettling in itself, and I have to believe it would have spawned my curiosity.

When I finally did feel the nudge to change, I joined a Bible study. I started attending church on a regular basis, and I read the Bible. The closer I drew to Jesus, the more peace I had. I started to crave time with Him.

Looking back, God had surrounded me with women of faith who stepped up to support me when my life was caving in. I remember breaking the devastating news to my Bible study, and within a couple of days, they rallied together and came to my house. We all sat on the sofa huddled together. They let me share my sorrow. They prayed for me. They were my support team. This is how God works. He had it all lined up for me.

Not only did I have my friends; I had my family that propped me up and gave me strength. They were not physically with me, but we would talk for hours and hours. My poor sister had to listen to my obsessive loops of worry almost on a daily basis. She would constantly remind me to focus on God's truths versus the facts of my circumstance. The idea is to take the focus off your circumstances and look at the truths that God has promised you.

For example, I would have said, "I'm all alone." But the truth was, God was always with me. I had two children, a very supportive family, and dear friends to lean on.

When I said "I cannot do this on my own," factually speaking, I was right. It was going to take some financial help and emotional support, but the God truth was, I could *do all things through Christ who strengthened me* (Philippians 4:13).

Bear in mind, pain has a tendency to overshadow God's blessings, and then we view our life from a defeatist perspective. Watch for the blessings that God has placed along your path, because they are easily overlooked.

Being the yoga teacher that I am, this brings me to a yoga analogy. When a student is in a balancing pose, concentration is necessary. The student must set her eyes on a focal point to maintain balance. If she focuses on a moving object, like another student, she will fall. Much like life, you have to fix your gaze on Christ, not your situation. The world around you is in flux, and when you set your eyes upon the circumstances, your head spins, making you dizzy and confused; balance is lost. Jesus is your rock, your focal point, constant and true. Set your gaze on Him when the environment around you is spinning out of control, and He will give you peace.

Finding peace during the dark days can be challenging. It may even seem like God is silent. The pain and suffering drive a person either to God or away from God. Undeniably, it drove me closer to God. My practice of daily devotions, journaling, and meditating contributed to my peaceful state of mind. I was finally cultivating a meaningful relationship with Christ, and it wasn't complicated. It was much easier than I ever believed it could be. It's simple to know God. All you have to do is seek Him, and He will show up for you.

The Apology

*I will refine them like silver and purify
them like gold.*
—Zechariah 13:9

*We are not doubting God will do the best for us;
we are wondering how painful the
best will turn out to be.*
—C. S. Lewis

When I was a little girl, we had a maid named Mary Kate. Mary Kate had witnessed two generations of my family grow up. She had also helped my family and our relatives raise kids, cook, and clean. She overcame childhood poverty, segregation, racism, and an abusive husband. She was a very wise black Southern woman.

I can vividly remember my mother's eyes with a furrowed brow looking into Mary Kate's face as they both stood cooking over a hot stove in the Georgia summer heat. My mother, in an abusive marriage herself, was intently listening to Mary Kate's sage advice when she couldn't understand my father's bad behavior. Mary Kate always told my mother, "What comes around goes around. It may be a long time coming, but it's coming."

Mary Kate's lesson is a message for us all. You may never see regret from your ex-spouse or hear the apology you always wanted, but you must know it's not your duty to seek it or wish vengeance on him. And it's not your job to understand it either. Understanding will come later.

Give yourself time to forgive. It took me years to do. As I was swinging between the spaces of *settling in* and *surrendering*, forgiveness showed up. When I could see that my resentment and anger against my ex was punishing me and only me, I made a shift in my walk. I started to see the transition of divorce as a refining process that God was taking me through.

In the beginning, the pain from the divorce was uncomfortable, and like anyone, I resisted it. I knew God had the best intentions for me, but I sure didn't welcome the brutal road that I had to endure in order to learn the lesson and to discover that the valley is a place of refinement and purification. It's in the fire or uneasiness of the valley where God does His best work. He refines you by burning off the impurities and extraneous garbage, allowing you to be a reflection of Himself.

It took me a while to see my situation as a refining process, but once I did, forgiveness quickly trailed behind. Forgiveness is optional, but bear in mind the endless supply of forgiveness God bestows upon you. Look at God's grace. He doesn't require we do something in order to receive His compassion, gentleness, and forgiveness. All we have to do is believe. He is wastefully extravagant with the love He pours on us. He loves us all—backsliders and all. Take a note from His book. It's your duty to find love, compassion, and gentleness toward your ex-spouse, which is the definition of grace. Eventually forgiveness will show up, because forgiveness walks hand in hand with grace. So shouldn't you do the same to your ex-husband?

Take into consideration, a man's bad behavior provides a glimpse of the pain he carries within. When you look at it this way, compassion shows up. Compassion says "I will walk alongside you in your pain." It's the virtue that quells anger and softens the heart, which opens the door to forgiveness.

How I Forgave My Ex

Forgiveness is the fragrance that the violet
sheds on the heel that has crushed it.
— Mark Twain

Ah yes, the dreaded act of "forgiveness." I talk to other women who have walked down this same road of divorce, and there's always hesitation when asked the question, have you forgiven him? That's a tough question to answer and a difficult feat to accomplish. I remember being asked the same question shortly after the divorce. I knew I hadn't forgiven him, and I knew I had to do it. I discovered that I had to heal the brokenness in my heart before I could even begin to think about forgiving the man who hurt me so deeply.

I ended up learning forgiveness from an unlikely source. I watched my mother display fierce compassion and forgiveness toward my father, who caused her a lot of suffering. For most of my life, my mother's resentment toward my father was palpable. My father was a severe alcoholic for twenty-plus years. He was emotionally and mentally cruel to my mother for as long as I can remember. There was also some physical abuse, but he favored verbal disparagement over anything else. As you can imagine, life was messy for my family, especially for my mother.

When I was fifteen, my father, a doctor, was forced into sobriety by the medical board. Finally, this was the change my mother had prayed for. She thought possibly they could salvage the marriage of thirty-eight years until she found out there was another woman. It happened to be the bookkeeper, and yes, she was skimming off the top of the family's money. Divorce was inevitable. Too much hurt and brokenness existed to mend the marriage. Quite frankly, it was shocking they had lasted as long as they did. After thirty-eight years of marriage, my parents finally separated and then two years later divorced.

A few years passed, and then my father was diagnosed with Alzheimer's. We children were not busting down doors to help because, honestly, he had been a crummy dad. One of my sisters did step up and take over to help my father in his early years of Alzheimer's. Eventually, he needed more care and had to go to a nursing home. That was when my mother showed me what it means to forgive by walking in the light of Christ. She would visit my father two to three times a week, driving thirty-five minutes both ways. She would feed him and bring him presents. He could no longer talk and was confined to a bed, and his hands had atrophied into two close-fisted mitts.

On her visits, my mother would take over the nurse's job and spoon-feed my father his meals. The woman who put up with twenty-plus years of abuse fed the source of all her pain, literally and figuratively. She was giving love and compassion to the person who caused the most damage in her life. In return, she received the gift of forgiveness. Oh, what a glorious gift it was! After forty years of resentment and bitterness, she finally forgave my father, dumping the heavy bag of burden.

The forgiveness healed her, and I know deep down, my father could feel the love, the total acceptance that he probably always craved. She was walking in love, as Christ did. It was a sacrifice that, in the end, brought light to the darkness of her soul. What was a chore ended up being the very thing she needed to heal her heart.

This was an act of healing between two damaged souls. In their old age, they both sat there as if the years of abuse had never existed. From the outside, no one would have ever known their story of pain, abuse, and dysfunction. Instead, a stranger in passing would have witnessed a woman feeding her husband with love. And that is exactly what it was—pure love, absent of all darkness and full of God's light!

Forgiveness is a choice. You are a creature of free will, so it will take serious effort on your part to generate forgiveness for your ex-spouse. Without forgiveness, you will remain stuck. Forgiveness will bring peace to your soul and alignment with the will of God. It is an integral component in your transition from *married* to *divorced*. Without it, you will not advance forward.

The opposite of forgiveness is not "unforgiveness." This word doesn't even exist. The opposite of forgiveness is anger. You know the saying *"Holding on to anger is like drinking poison and expecting the other person to die."* When we carry anger, we pollute our spirit, mind, and body, creating a perfect environment for disease. This could manifest itself into an illness of the physical body or sickness of the mind. You must actively participate in keeping healthy from the inside out, including your mental health as well as your physical state.

The Bible implies that, *we must command our thoughts.* Controlling your mental activity in normal everyday life is already difficult, and then when you add a messy breakup to the mix, the mind goes topsy-turvy with runaway thoughts. You know the kind—wishing bad things on your ex, then taking them back, then thinking maybe a little bit of misery wouldn't be such a terrible thing. He hurt you after all, so why should he get away scot-free? Don't drink the poison! This is the poison that will only harm you.

To forgive means to set yourself free from the bondage of resentment, anger, and hate by bringing light to the darkness of the soul. It requires that you actively cultivate forgiveness, discipline, and fierce compassion. What you watch, say to others, daydream about, and listen to feeds your thoughts, which translates into your actions. You have to make a conscious effort to nourish your mind much like you do with your body.

An experienced marathon runner will not be a cigarette-smoking athlete who eats a breakfast of chocolate donuts before the big race. Obviously, the empty calories would not give the athlete the energy to run twenty-six miles. So when we feed our brains with junk, why are we surprised when it leaves us with a negative frame of mind?

The series *Breaking Bad* won a slew of prestigious awards back in 2014. Out of curiosity, I wanted to see what all the hype was about. After watching two shows, I had restless, disturbing dreams. I realized watching a show about the brutal and violent life of manufacturing and selling methamphetamine right before bed is a bad idea. It makes sense, right?

Undoubtedly, the negative visuals I put into my head fed the darkness of my state of mind. Obviously, you can shut off outside sources like the television, but how do you control negative thoughts within your own head? It's easy to get stuck on a mental loop of gloom, rehearsing made-up scenarios that most likely will never occur. I have been guilty of fast-forwarding to the worst possible outcome and then being pleasantly surprised that the results were not remotely like the nightmare that I had conceived in my head.

When you do this, you are experiencing unnecessary stress many times over. In order to stop creating pointless stress, you must actively take the reins of that runaway horse, a.k.a. your mind, and reel it back in. When thoughts wander to the dark places, direct your mind to a place of gratitude, a place of positivity.

This translates to reading, watching, or listening to material that nourishes your soul. It's making a list of blessings. It's praying and meditating on God, taking the focus off you and lifting your face toward Him. It's being more like Jesus and praying for the person(s) who have hurt you. Try it! It's hard to hate a person you are praying for.

It's being aware of the words you speak, especially the words that follow "I am." The tongue, much like a rudder on a large ship, directs your path. If you are verbalizing self-defeating thoughts, then expect a dissatisfied life.

If you're saying "I am too poor to afford such and such," you're reinforcing poverty. Verbalizing it leads to developing, shaping, and forming the condition. The good news is, it's easy to fix. Simply say "Now is not the time to buy that," reinforcing that later there will be a time to purchase it. This can go far beyond money. It can be used to describe your state of being.

Forgiveness also includes forgiving yourself for the divorce. When you view your divorce as a failure, you are not trusting that

God *works for the good of those who love him.* You are under the assumption that you are in complete control.

Or just maybe your God is not big enough. I heard once that if He is a god that's small enough for your brain to comprehend, then He is not big enough to meet your needs. Just know, God is so big that you cannot fathom the abundance He wants to provide for you, nor do you know what His plan is for you. Instead of seeing this divorce as an epic failure, look at it as your second chance to make your life what God intended it to be. At times, it may seem like divorce is some form of punishment, but think, just maybe God extracted you from the triviality of your life so you could reach your full potential. It's not a demotion but rather a promotion where God is lifting you up to be closer to Him.

This requires you to discard the negative thoughts of failure and abandonment with thoughts of abundance and gratitude. A mental shift must occur to move you out of the darkness into the light, becoming more like Jesus. And isn't that the goal anyway? Ask yourself, *What would Jesus do right now if He were walking down my same path?* He would forgive, love his neighbor and enemies as himself. So get to it. This is going to require a major shift in your perspective, perhaps a complete upheaval!

Mom and Dad circa 1950

Spiritually Bankrupt

God whispers to us in our pleasure, speaks in
our consciences, but shouts in our pains. It is
his megaphone to rouse a deaf world.
—C. S. Lewis

Unfortunately, there are many people out there who are spiritually bankrupt. Faith is a necessary component in the walk of life. When faith is missing, the God-sized hole grows and expands. I knew an extreme example of a God-sized hole in a man. He had a beautiful family, a loving wife, two children, a comfortable home, and a nice-paying job. He turned to his wife one day and said, "Is this it? Because if it is, I should go ahead and end it all now." The man was empty, devoid of God. His God-sized hole was gaping wide open, so much so that he had become a walking outline of a human being. He needed God so desperately, but he continued to fill the void with more worldly possessions. He based his self-worth on how much money he made, what house he lived in, and what car he drove. He looked to his wife to bring him happiness when there was no possible way she could ever achieve this undertaking. The answer was very clear to the people of faith, but he chose to continue searching for the next best thing that would bring him fleeting happiness.

Does this story sound familiar? Maybe it is your ex-husband who has strayed from God, or maybe it is you. It doesn't take some grand production to rekindle a relationship with God. Seek Him and He will show up. God asks that you come as you are, sinner and all. There's no prerequisite to be a follower of Christ. That's the beauty of God's grace. If God were to write a letter to a backslider or someone who has never had a relationship with Christ, I believe it would go something like this.

> *Dear wanderer,*
>
> *Come home. You're not too far. Life did not unfold exactly like you had in mind. Reality is not what you expected. I will always be here for you. Lay down your hurt, lay down your shame. Come as you are—broken—and come to me. There's so much more to be had than the material world you worship. I know everything about you. Nothing you have done or will do can separate you from me. You are one of the many lost children walking this earth, but I am your true Father. You are my beloved, and you are enough. I want to teach you, love you. I want you to know me. I am not some abstract being. Anyone can know me. All they have to do is call out my name. I am the Father, the Son, and the Holy Ghost. Call out to me, and I will answer. I am right here, and I have been waiting for you.*
>
> *Love,*
> *Jesus*

Jesus gave us two instructions to follow, and He emphasized "there is no commandment greater than these." You'd think we wouldn't have such a hard time following direction, but we do. First, He said, "Love the Lord with all your heart, and with all your soul, and with all your mind and with all your strength" (Mark 12:30).

In the marriage, I was guilty of not making God the center of my world, which was a form of not loving Him completely. God was like a hobby of mine that I dabbled in only when it was convenient, which disregards the first rule Jesus gave us.

The second instruction is "to love your neighbor"—your ex-husband—"as yourself." If you are still reeling from the divorce, I can understand the enormity of what this asks of you, but I know you can find some space in your heart for compassion. This is a form of love. Choose to hate the behavior, not the person.

Be sure to look at the whole picture, like the family background. In my case, it helped me see where we both came from. Both being children of divorce, my ex-husband and I didn't have healthy examples to follow. My ex-husband's parents had seven divorces between the two of them. I was a child of divorce and a child of alcoholism, and so was he. *What did we know about marriage?* Our divorce could have been predicted by statistics alone. We both came from two worlds of "spectacular dysfunction."

I'm at a place now where I can honestly say I love my ex-husband. I love him without expectation. He still gets me riled up, but when I love, not expecting a thing in return, I'm following God's instructions. I look at the grace God has given me and think it is only fair I extend grace to my ex-husband. So as I sit here, I am troubled by a future court date that hangs over my head. During times of strife, it's difficult to muster love, per se, but I can find compassion and understanding. And I know this hiccup shall pass. It will pass and soon be a distant memory. When my ex and I have conflict between us, I treat it like a business deal. When I take away the emotion from the situation, I can be around him and still treat him with respect. My children see it, and that's the most important objective.

Recently, we had to go to a parent-teacher meeting together, and I'm sure by the looks of it, we seemed like we had an ideal relationship as exes. We were laughing and telling stories of our past; little did anyone know we have a court date on the books.

It's not always a walk in the park with my ex. I use verses to soothe my anxiety flare-ups. It's like having a set of tools in my back pocket. I repeat the hymn "It Is Well with My Soul," and it's amazing how these simple words can alter my state of being, from *anxious* to *faithful*. Music can be and should be used as a comfort. In fact, I wrote the letter "Dear Wanderer" after hearing the inspirational lyrics to David Crowder's "Come As You Are." Another favorite lyric of mine is, "I will climb this mountain with my hands wide open," by the Mike Clark Band (originally by Will Reagan and United Pursuit).

I am a firm believer that *energy flows where intention goes.* As you meditate on words of strength, you are setting your intention and mind-set for the day. Thoughts create energy, which yields intention and results in action.

Here are some words of strength to make your own:

> "I lean not on my own understanding, my life is in the hands of the Maker of Heaven." (The Mike Clark Band)
>
> "I give it all to you God, trusting that'll you make something beautiful out of me." (The Mike Clark Band)
>
> "I will climb this mountain with my hands wide open." (The Mike Clark Band)
>
> "If God is for us, who can be against us?" (Romans 8:31)
>
> "A life rooted in Christ stands firm." (Proverbs 12:3)
>
> "I can do all things through Christ who strengthens me." (Philippians 4:13)

Thanksgiving Grace

*You will never reach your destination if you stop
and throw stones at every dog that barks.*
　　　　　　　　　—Winston S. Churchill

*Pick your battles. You don't have to show up
to every argument you're invited to.*
　　　　　　　　　—Mandy Hale

In today's society, *to surrender* implies weakness. My hope is that you will view surrendering differently. Regard your *surrender* phase as an adjustment period. It's choosing the path that Jesus Himself would take, aligning yourself with God's will, not your own. It's about finding grace when you are tempted to be graceless.

When I was married, Thanksgiving was my jam. Most of our kinfolks are in Georgia, so my husband and I had to create a new tradition when we moved to California. We used to host elaborate Thanksgiving dinners, inviting our friends who were also fellow transplants of the community. We pulled out the china and silver and set up long tables with white linens and beautiful floral arrangements.

Divorce changed this tradition drastically. Somehow I lost Thanksgiving, and the friends.

Now my ex-husband hosts Thanksgiving parties that resemble small carnivals, with teacup-style amusement rides and bouncy houses to boot. Naturally, my kids want to ditch my no-frills Thanksgiving to go join the fun.

In the past, I have been tempted to pitch a holy tantrum and shout "shenanigans" at the unfairness of it all, but instead, I swallow my pride and give up my children for the day. Some battles are not worth the fight.

I have discovered that finding the grace to move beyond the emotional snags makes my life easier and much less stressful. Life is about change, and I know deep down the Thanksgivings with the dancing bears and flying unicorns will not last. My kids will grow up, and the shiny, sparkly attractions will lose their luster.

The reality is, I have the right to host my own Thanksgiving party, and I have chosen not to, for now. But who's to say that won't change? Just maybe next year, I will throw the family a curveball and host my Thanksgiving on a Saturday in January.

Thanksgiving is just a day that we have assigned sentiment to, so what does it matter if I pick another day for the celebration? Oftentimes, we divorced parents get caught up in power struggles, and the answer simply lies in finding the creativity to redesign the situation. It's an adjustment, and it's okay if it doesn't resemble what your *normal* used to look like.

We must step back from the issue to see what's getting in the way. When I look at the whole picture, I can see I have my children the majority of the time. I'm in the nitty-gritty, the nooks and crannies of their lives, and I know I'm not missing out on a thing.

It's what seems to be the negligible times that are so crucial in raising children, like the downtime, the conversations to and from school when I hear the substance of their lives. The fleeting, sparkly celebrations do not hold a candle to the importance of day-to-day living. The daily living is the bread and butter of child rearing, and it's extremely tedious. It's a long race to raise children to be decent, moral adults, and you may not see the prize for years, but you gotta "run, Forrest, run!"

The daily grind is wearisome and anything but glamorous, but it's paramount that you and I are in the game. When they are young, you are physically exhausted from their daily cycle of "feed, play, sleep, repeat." But as the kids enter into the teen years, the social and academic struggles are, hands down, the most energy-zapping emotional drains. The saying "Bigger kids, bigger problems" hits it on the mark. Watching the social dynamics of a teenage girl is enough to make a person question mankind altogether, because fourteen-year-old girls can be satanic beasts.

And then there's the insanely high demand on us parents to help our children perform well academically. As a kid, I never had any help with my homework, unless it was an art project, then my mother took it on like it was her job. It was above and beyond what the teacher required, and I (my mother) always made an A+.

As a teen, if I had asked my mother to help me with a math problem, she would have laughed in my face. She simply didn't have time for that, nor did she have a clue how to do it. Now I find myself relearning sixth-grade math so I can then reteach it to my daughter. It usually involves some bizarre breakdown of a problem that can be done in three different ways. In my day, there was only one way to solve the equation, and that happened to be the easiest path to take. Today's math is not math of yesteryear, that's for sure. So what do I do? I adjust and relearn.

Along the same lines, now that you are divorced, I'm advising you to readjust and relearn a new way to do things. Start by picking grace over gracelessness. It's basic problem solving that can usually be done several different ways. Many times, the solution happens to be taking the path of least resistance if it's an inconsequential matter like my *surrendered Thanksgiving*. Pick your battles wisely, my friend. If in the long run it's not going to have much significance, well then, you know the answer.

To most of the world, this stance could be viewed as weak, but I see it as an evolution to a higher level of being. You have chosen to not partake in the hollowness of life, because you know where the importance lies. These small submissions are choices to free yourself from the emotional snares that can easily entangle you. It's a sign of great advancement when you learn how to pick and choose the substance of life. This is a time of aligning yourself to be more godly. These small but significant choices will make it possible to rise above the madness of divorce.

Exercise I: God Truths

What is your biggest fear right now?

What do you consider a risk right now?

What is holding you back?

What is your gut telling you?

In the left column below, jot down the "untruths" that you continue to tell yourself. In the right column, apply the God-truths to counter the negative self-talk.

For example:

My life is over.   *My marriage is ending, not my life.*

Exercise II: Finding God in the Valley

List some battles that you are willing to give up.

How do you see your situation as a refining process?

What steps have you made that reflect an *alignment* with God?

Where do you believe you are in the forgiveness process?

Part IV

The Gift

The saying "God will never give you more than you can handle" used to throw me into a fuming tailspin, and I would think, *Judging by the heaping pile of mess stacked on top of me, God must think I'm a rock star.* The truth is, God will give you more than *you think* you can handle, but He will be there to bring you through it. I slogged through the valley, and God brought me all the way through and out the other side. Toward the tail end, I found a gift. The gift was purpose, and *knowing why I was doing what I was doing* changed the course of my life. Having purpose gave me the extra stamina needed to continue the slog all the way through the valley. I discovered contentment follows a purpose-driven life, and that's what this chapter is about.

We have discussed the different phases of transition: *entering the valley, settling in, and surrendering.* Now let's look at *the gift.* In this phase, you will receive the gift of direction after hoofing it through the valley. If you haven't reached this point yet, be excited about the day that will come when you discover your purpose.

Purpose will lead you out of the valley and up into the hills for clarity. Finally, you will look down and see the path you have traveled, but now you will possess a newfound appreciation for the journey itself.

My wish is for you to see how necessary this trip was in order to find the gift of purpose. I discovered I couldn't have found purpose without first experiencing pain, and you may discover that too.

God's presence was in the valley, and as I reached the homestretch, His presence was even more apparent, because I had tapped into a purpose-driven life directed by His will.

Forcing Fruit

Bloom where you are planted.
—1 Corinthians 7:20–24

I just cleaned out my desk, and I came across a picture of my youngest daughter in kindergarten—a heart-shaped baby face with wide baby blues peering into the camera. The split second captured in time, now gone forever. Then it hit me; this picture was taken right before the storm hit. It was probably taken in the fall or winter before the ugly spring—my ugly spring, that is. I think about my precious angels and what we put them through: the stress of brokenness, the stress of seeing their mother wilt and become a puddle on the floor. Oh, my poor babies, wanting so badly to make me happy. Looking back, this divide between my ex-husband and me left a deep scar in all of us. If I had to guess, it even left a scar in him. So many hearts ached over this divide, not just me *(journal entry 2012)*.

The transition we take from married to divorced is an emotional whirlwind that breaks us wide open. The cracks of the soul are left behind after the trauma and show our brokenness, but God loves broken things. He uses our brokenness to carry out his will. The scar left behind is the opening where the light of God can enter. It's your badge of honor that says you survived. It will be the symbol of strength that got you through divorce.

Out of pain, there will be purpose. God has given you this burden for a reason, and He does not target the superstars of society to carry the load. Just look at the motley crew of broken men Jesus called to be His disciples. Before they were disciples, this group of men were not particularly gifted, except maybe at fishing, but not as spiritual leaders. They were called by Christ to follow Him. They did not seek their calling.

The soil is rich in the valley, and your troubles are like bits and pieces of the compost pile. This pile of smelly refuse becomes rich fertilizer to nourish new growth, taking the mess and turning it into the message. The garbage that got you here serves as the catalyst needed to support your growth. And if you are fortunate, this "stirring up" leads to the discovery of your *calling*, but do not let that word intimidate you.

Oftentimes, I found myself getting wrapped around the axle because I didn't know what my calling was. In truth, it's just a label. A calling sounds like a daunting task that must be tackled, but a gift is nonthreatening. Think about when someone gives you a present; you graciously receive it, with no pressure, and willfully accept it, possibly with glee. It's a natural and comfortable transaction. But when we replace the word *calling* with *gift*, it then becomes less of a threat and a more doable undertaking.

I want to emphasize that I did not go out and discover my talent. God revealed it to me. God called me to do this work. I never would have signed up for a position with the job description "Seeking a devoted wife and mother who is willing to get emotionally reamed to find her purpose-driven life." Let's face it; no one wants to experience the pain, because we are shortsighted beings. Many times, we can only see what is in front of us and nothing beyond our present circumstance. Rarely do we anticipate the future growth that the present-day pain will yield.

If someone had told me in my twenties that *divorce support* would be my gift, it would have sent me running away from the altar. It certainly wouldn't have motivated me to ever marry, but God has a peculiar way of placing burdens on you to make you bear fruit.

Every December, I force flowers to bloom; I buy bulbs, place them in a vase with rocks, water them, and then voilà, I have fragrant blooming paperwhites at Christmas, and that's exactly what God did to me in the valley. What I thought would be a dormant season in my life, God had something different in mind. He forced me to blossom, to find my fruit in the harsh terrain of the valley.

During the marriage, I had osmosed into my husband. His likes were my likes. We did the things he wanted to do. We had fallen into traditional gender roles, not on purpose, but because it was easy. I handled the kids, the meals, the house, and basically everything except the businesses. He was building a career, and I was facilitating it. I never thought to try my hand at anything other than my role as his wife and mother to our girls. The sad part is, I let my husband's life become more valuable than my own. I had lost my way, my uniqueness.

When he walked out the door, my shelter had been taken away. No longer could I hide in the shadow of my husband. God gave me the "holy kick in the pants" to remove the obstacle that blocked my expansion. I didn't want this big, scary change. It seemed like more than I could handle, but God didn't seem to think so. Divorce was bleak, and I wanted no part of it.

My divorce was ugly, period. But isn't every dismantlement of a family unit ugly? The aftershock ripped through my family and even affected the periphery, dissolving friendships, and I was left to clean up the wreckage of my life.

I am an artist, and naturally, my emotions come through my artwork. It's therapeutic and meditative for me to sit and lose myself while painting, sculpting, creating. During this painful time, I made a collage where my ex-husband was a pile of bits and pieces of stacked limbs, dismantled and fragmented. My two daughters and I stood looking out over the heap of rubble—the mess that was stacked in front of me. We were gazing to the future. The entire work of art is covered with words of pain, making swirls and shapes with text. It's raw and represented suffering, wreckage, and chaos. It isn't a pretty picture, and it has a Holocaust feel to it. I kept this piece because it shows and continues to show me how far I have come. It shows me that I did pick up the pieces of my life, and along the walk, I found purpose, and I gained wisdom. God had something much bigger in store for me.

Divorce was a daunting project, but I was there to discover something much larger than I ever could have imagined. I was there in the valley to discover who I was supposed to be and what I was supposed to be doing. God was forcing me to grow, expand, and blossom.

It took being cracked wide open to discover the gift within, and the fall of the marriage was God's way of *forcing fruit* to reveal my God-given talent.

Who knew I would come out of the valley with a newfound purpose? It was not until the tail end of the trek that I discovered my gift. Many days, I contemplated my life, knowing I was meant to be on this earth for something much larger than what I had going on, but I didn't know exactly what that was. Not all of us are privy to the gift(s) God has given us, even though each of us has one or a few, and not all of us are ready to embrace our gift(s).

If you're on the hunt or contemplating your purpose, try something—on your next project or new opportunity, look at your life through a different lens. Take a spiritual approach rather than a needy "What will make me happy?" MO. Ask, *What can I do that will bring more joy to this world?* Creating a purpose-driven life is the answer, but first, you have to find your gift. When you invite God into the gift-finding process, you will get that much closer to its discovery. This is an act of creating something larger than yourself, taking the emphasis off you as an egocentric being and putting the emphasis on you as a child of God. The shift is a game changer, because when we serve, we are blessed. And if you are seeking a gift from this perspective, you will truly be a reflection of God.

Start with these questions:

> What charges you? What can you see doing even if you didn't get paid to do it?
>
> What could you do all day long and be content?
>
> How does God fit into the scenario?

Do not get bogged down with what the *gift* is. It doesn't have to be something grandiose. It may be as simple as being a great mom capable of cooking dinner, responding to the barrage of school e-mails while simultaneously teaching common core math to your child. God does not rate gifts. Being a great mom is just as important as being a medical missionary in Kenya. You may not have a clue what your God-given talent is, and it's okay. It can be as simple as being an exceptional friend or possessing the gift of prayer or the gift to raise children with patience.

If you don't have an inkling what your gift may be, wait for it. You may not be ready yet. I had to wait for it myself. There's no way I could have written this book before now. I was too raw and hurt, and if I had written an earlier version, it would have been more appropriately titled *Jilted and Desperate*. I worked on myself, and I discovered some talents along the way. Most importantly, I became a stronger Christian, and maybe that was what God wanted all along.

In the height of pain, you see what is truly important. When times are good, we have a tendency to forget how much we need our Father, but when times are bad, we call out His name. Maybe that is what God wants of you; He may be calling you to be a better Christian.

No matter where you are on this journey, when the day comes and your gift, your fruit, is revealed to you, do not hide it. Share it! Pay it forward. That's your purpose. Consider it a mission from God. You're producing fruit for others to enjoy. If you're truly walking in the fruit of the spirit with goodness in your heart, God will reveal your gift. You are then driven to share it with the world. What a beautiful thing this is! And the best part is, God has given each and every one of us unique spiritual gifts.

A Moment of Sudden Revelation

Now I will show you what I will do.
—Exodus 6:1

In my opinion, no word is powerful enough to describe my state of mind when the collapse of my marriage happened. I could fill up this page with adjectives of desperation and still not adequately illustrate my emotional state at that juncture in my life. I turned to my faith and a daily practice of yoga. Both practices allowed me to escape from reality for an hour when I did not have to focus on the demise of my marriage. I could listen to a sermon, or I could become lost in a pose or meditation. It was in yoga class when God revealed my first gift to me.

I remember going to a shishi yoga studio with its predictable statue of Shiva greeting visitors at the door. There were also tapestries of the elephant god Ganesha and random Buddhas used as decoration for the space. Why is it that most yoga studios feel compelled to show-case Hindu gods and different types of Buddhas as if it's a prerequisite for only the *legit* studios? God forbid, if we ever brought Jesus into the mix, then we would be accused of trying to push Christianity down the throats of the yogis, but for some reason, other gods are accept-able. Ironically, there's a running argument that yoga isn't religious.

Yogis typically have an affinity for a *coexist* philosophy, so it shouldn't offend anyone to have an *all-or-nothing attitude* when it comes to what religious symbols are represented in a yoga studio. As you can tell, I feel strongly about this subject, and it just so happens to be apropos to my first gift, which was revealed to me in a *new age* yoga class.

The class began, and things were already starting to get weird. The teacher looked like a fusion of an eighties aerobics instructor mixed with a Hindu Sikh. She asked if there were any new people, and I raised my hand. At this point, there was no turning back. People had seen me. I was stuck, and the man in front of me was grinning from ear to ear like he knew something I didn't. Then the instructor started talking about Bob the builder. I didn't quite understand where she was going with this, but she somehow tied it into her new house renovations. We then started moving into sun salutations, and she urged us to awaken the goddess from within. I looked to my neighbor for support, but he too seemed a little freaked out. We wrapped up the class by clumsily chanting in Sanskrit. I'm certain no one knew the meaning of the chant, except maybe our instructor and the toothy guy in front.

That day, in that studio, with its hokey goddess-awakening performance, a light bulb went off, and I realized yoga didn't have to be a *new age* practice that made Christians feel excluded. No longer did yoga need to make *anyone* feel they had to convert religions before they could partake. It was this aha moment when I realized I had the ability and influence to transform yoga for the Christian community.

Yoga is an extremely spiritual practice, and it heals. It got me through my dark days. I knew by incorporating prayer and recognizing God as part of the yoga experience; I could encourage Christians to practice, making it a comfortable and an inviting experience.

I had always been a yoga student, never the instructor, so I earned my certification and started a company called Faithful Warrior. It's what saved me during the walk across the valley of divorce. It gave me purpose, and I was more than happy to share this practice with other Christians.

In a typical yoga class, the last pose symbolizes a *death-to-rebirth* experience. If you're not familiar with final relaxation, it's at the end of the yoga practice where the student surrenders and lets go to find complete stillness and peace. The idea is to shed the old self to become new. The metamorphosis that divorce takes you through represents just that—a death of the old self to the birth of the new self.

God was doing just that—making me new. He was showing me who I was. India, the woman that did not know her core values, that defined herself through her husband and children, the woman that had no passion, and the woman who did not know her own strength, shed her skin in the valley.

I died in the valley and became new through Christ. God made divorce, with all its shame and ugliness, into a beautiful thing. Now that I have exited the valley, I look up to heaven and know God rescued me. He removed me from a passionless life. He saw the potential that I did not know I possessed. My life needed to unfold as it did so I could find my gifts to share with the world. I am convinced this is His plan for you too.

Walking through the Valley
with Children in Tow

If you want to change the world,
go home and love your family.
—Mother Teresa

A s the marital separation was morphing into divorce, life did not stop. There were still early morning school drop-offs, afternoon sports, dental appointments, and birthday parties. Actually, this was a blessing. As much as I wanted to, I could not put life on hold as I sank deeper into my pain. I had to be a mother to my children, who were hurting too. Their grades, physical health, and behavior reflected the stress at home.

Bottom line—divorce impacts children, without question. I so often hear people say children are resilient and can get through divorce. Children get through divorce much like an amputee gets over the loss of a limb. Sure, they can manage life, but there will always be a wound they carry with them. And if they had the choice, they would like to have the severed limb still attached. Or in a case like mine, most children would prefer to have their father still part of the family unit.

Children are watching you to see how to do *adulting*. Do not take this role lightly.

Rules to Follow

1. Always remain the parent. Do not blur the lines; complaining to your kids about their father is unacceptable. Save those chats for a girlfriend or a therapist. Be an example and teach your children how to love. Follow the greatest commandments given to us: "Love the Lord your God with all your heart and love your neighbor as yourself" (Mark 12:30–31).
2. Set boundaries. It's easier to have loose limits because boundaries have to be enforced. If consequences are threatened and not executed, kids will prey on this weakness every chance they get. And then you become a pushover.
3. Lose the guilt for being a divorcée. This is where you are. Stop regretting and start learning how to teach your child how to become a godly man or woman.
4. Do not abandon your children. "Abandon" you say! Why, I'd never! And it may seem like an inflammatory word. In a crisis, like divorce, you become an egocentric being, even when you have children dependent on you. It's as if you don't have enough bandwidth to meet anyone else's needs but your own. You may be a very likable, generous person, but when you are stressed to the max, you are less capable of being a good, solid parent. I myself lost pockets of time for being too self-absorbed in my own calamity. I thank the good Lord I had earthly angels to pick up where I was lacking. If abandonment continues, children look to their peers to find solace. If in adolescence, it may result in attention-driven behavior such as drug/alcohol abuse or

sexual promiscuity. They need to be valued and cherished by you. Engage your children, and let them know you are available to them. Waste time with them. Talk about the mundane. Ask open-ended questions. Be silly.

5. Show a child he is good enough because he is a child of God, not because he is a star athlete or she is an above-average student. Understand, life as a kid today can be unbearable. They want to feel safe, and you have the ability to create this for them. Clothe yourself with compassion for your child.

6. Listen. Children grieve too, and they need to be heard. Therapy is an excellent way for children to open up about things they may not feel comfortable talking about with you. Children need other adults to parent them in addition to you. Aunts, uncles, grandparents, or trusted friends will take pride in helping you raise your child. "It takes a village" philosophy really is necessary. When I was little, other neighborhood mothers had no problem scolding me. Now we are walking around scared to offend, giving people so much space we are becoming isolated beings. Today it's quite possible to live next door to a neighbor for ten years and never know his name, but don't let this discourage you. Begin by lining up friends and family members who can mentor your child. Share the responsibility with others.

7. Do not rush dating. No need to hurry the process. When a boyfriend enters the scene too quickly, it confuses children. They are forced to redefine the family unit while they are still reeling from the breakup of *family* as they knew it. It's a selfish act. If you feel ready to date, do so, but leave the children out of it. When you do introduce the new man to your children and they don't welcome your love interest with open arms, *do not* force it. Instead, acknowledge they need more time. They may even show hostility toward him. To a child, the new man is *not Daddy*, and having any kind of a relationship with a man can seem like a betrayal

to their father. Don't get upset by it; instead, allow space and time.

8. Be understanding. Life is hard for the average adolescent, and divorce stacks more stress on top of an already-complicated phase of life.

9. Be a coach. "Train up a child in the way he should go; even when he is old he will not depart from it" (Proverbs 22:6). As children grow, you set and adjust their limits; when they are on their own, they will know the direction to take. Don't separate spiritual development from human development. Not only are you training a child to be a responsible adult; you are also training your child to be godly, which is the utmost virtue of human development.

In Latin, the word *resilient* translates to "leap again." As a parent, it's your duty to build yourself back up and leap again. At times, you may find yourself in the pits, but how great it is to know you have a bigger purpose—your child. Your child needs a trainer, and you fit that role. So get ready to jump and leap and laugh, living a fully engaged life with your children.

Hawaii 2015

It's Going to Leave a Mark

The burden is transformed into a pair of wings through the miracle of trust, and the one who is weighted down "will soar on wings like eagles."
—Isaiah 40:31, from
Sunday School Times

The Bible is chock-full of goodness. It's the rage to post inspirational quotes on different social media platforms, and sometimes it's cornball philosophy, but occasionally, there are gems that come rolling through my feed. Most of the time, the good ones can be traced back to the Bible. Funny thing is, the Bible has been giving us inspiration for centuries. I guess it could be called the first self-help book, but self-help implies we don't need God's help, and we both know we cannot do life alone. When we find ourselves in the *in-between* moments and God pushes the pause button on life, pulling ourselves up by the bootstraps just doesn't cut it. If you're anything like me, my funk was so deep there's no way I alone had the strength to "self-help" my way out of that black hole of despair. I resisted the major shift that was happening in my life. I wrestled with it like Jacob in Genesis, proving stories from the Bible are still applicable even in today's modern times.

In the first chapter of the Bible, a dysfunctional family enters the scene with its roll call of characters: Isaac, the passive father; Rebekah, the manipulative mother; Esau, the woolly older twin; and Jacob, the smooth-skinned younger twin. Jacob and Esau perpetuated a contemptuous relationship, and it looked as if the strife began from beginning. Jacob's name meant "holder of the heel," which is the polite way of saying "dirty, sneaky thief," and Esau meant "hairy." Both of the unfortunate names gave us a hint of what followed thereafter. In those days, the firstborn male was given advantages over the other children, but Esau had an extremely hard time holding on to his. First, he gave up his birthright to Jacob over a bowl of stew, and the second time, Jacob tricked his father into believing he was Esau. As a result, Esau lost his father's blessing, and this family confirmed dysfunction has been with us since the beginning of time—Genesis, to be exact.

Even though, God had made big promises to Jacob, Jacob couldn't relinquish control. Not only did he want to be in control; he was a restless control freak. God paid him a visit in a dream, and it wasn't a peaceful *heart-to-heart*. It was a wrestling match where God wouldn't let him go. Jacob wanted to control the situation, thinking he knew better than God.

I know this form of control all too well, like when I asked God to restore my very broken marriage. God knew the best outcome, and I didn't. Like Jacob, we have to surrender or forever be in God's choke hold. Once Jacob leaned into God and gave in, God left Jacob forever lamed. Isn't that what a transition is all about? Many times, it's the crippling that brings us to our knees to surrender so that God can do His best work. It's as if God has to wipe your slate clean so you then can be open to fully receive Him.

Before you were altered by divorce, maybe you were not capable of having the intimate relationship God desired. It might have been your ego or the comfortable lifestyle that kept you at a distance from Him. But there's nothing like a big crisis to shake you to the core, waking you from your spiritual slumber and launching you into a transition.

A transition is going to sting, and it's going to leave a mark. I'm forever altered from my heart being cracked wide open, but the crippling was the blessing. I wrestled with the change, fighting the transition from *married* to *divorced*. It took my heart being pried wide open to surrender to God and discover my true self. I was desperate to know God at this point in my life.

I will always look back on the early days of divorce as being super painful but extremely intimate with God. The discomfort was necessary to bring me through what I believe to be a sacred transition. It was sacred, because now I get to do this life, and I'm quite fond of it.

I wish God had renamed me like He did Jacob after his sacred transition. He became Israel, and I became *dependent on God*. People often ask me what my name means, and the truth is, as boring as it sounds, it's derived from the country of India, but if I had my druthers, it would mean "dependent on God," and it makes for a better story anyway. When I lived *independent of God*, I didn't know how to truly live with the greatness of Christ in me. Now I look at life with an entirely new set of eyes. I see beauty even in tragedy, because greatness comes out of the transitions in life.

As a result, we may be left with a hitch in our giddy-up or have a heart that has been cracked wide open, but this just makes room to love that much deeper—to love the broken, the sick, and the lost. But you can bet your life, it's going to leave a mark.

Not only will divorce leave a mark on you; it will leave its impression on your children too. My oldest child, Nora, is thirteen, and lately, we have had moments of conflict. It's to be expected, but there seems to be a constant argument orbiting around her cell phone. On one of these typical days, I pointed out that her drama level had reached a new all-time high and that if we were using the Homeland Security terror meter, she would be in the red zone. She quickly pointed out it's impossible for her not to jump to the worst-case scenario after the day I told her Dad was away on business and then he never came home. Her words knocked the wind out of me and pierced me to the core. I wanted to say "What choice did I have? You were eight, and your sister was six years old. How could I possibly explain something that I didn't understand myself?" The reality was, I was buying time to make sure the divorce was really going to happen.

But Nora was right; my casual explanation morphed into a gigantic life-altering experience for her. Once I knew it was definitely moving into divorce, I told my kids the truth, but her comment made me realize we identify that one moment in time that earmarks our pain. My blasé answer pinpointed the beginning of a profound shift in her world. The day I heard my husband say "It's over" stamped my timeline, as did the day I learned that the use of my words that were intended to protect actually harmed my child, branding her timeline too. These markers of pain scar the soul and can be viewed as the brutality of the human experience.

But what appears brutal can actually be a beautiful thing. Now, my daughters have an excellent ability to read all kinds of people, providing an education that cannot be learned at school. Navigating sticky situations is just part of it. In the two families alone, my daughters deal with four different adults, all with very different belief systems and personalities. Sure, we have been forever altered, but it was the brokenness that forced us to rely on God; now we have skills that can be used throughout a lifetime. What started out as a crippling experience left us beautifully altered and hand-shaped by God.

The Thank-You Note

Generally, by the time you are Real, most of your hair has been loved off, and your eyes drop out and you get loose in the joints and very shabby. But these things don't matter at all, because once you are Real you can't be ugly, except to people who don't understand.

—Margery Williams,
The Velveteen Rabbit

Dear Ex,

 Thank you for being the catalyst that catapulted me into a life that I love. At first, I wanted no part of its uncertainty. It was scary stepping out on my own. I was entering a vast new land of independence. Yoga and church were my sanctuary as I walked through the valley of divorce. I was healing my broken heart through yoga and through God, and I combined the two. Faithful Warrior Christian Yoga has been such a lifesaver. It gave me purpose and has launched me into other ventures, like writing this book. I never would have done this in my previous life with you. In a way, I was walking a treadmill life, very predictable, until the collapse of our marriage.

 The problem was, I was only living for you and the children. I didn't have anything that I could

109

call my own. And we both know children grow up and, obviously, marriages can fail. Divorce, in all its ugliness, forced me to discover a beautiful, God-given talent. My life now has meaning. I know I am here on this planet to guide women on the walk through the valley of divorce with grace and dignity. I have discovered God places us in *the middle of the storm to teach us*. And we have to set our sails directly into the storm, trusting the one that has commanded the squall.

I'll take the broken ones, battle-scarred and weary from divorce, and I will help them rebuild and create a life renewed. I know I can, because I did. And without you, I would not know this, nor would I have this gift to share.

My spiritual life, once dormant and asleep, is now awake and thriving because of you. I'm fully aware a life without meaning translates to restlessness; I know that feeling all too well from my past, but now my soul is at peace. Thank you for helping me make my life so full, meaningful, and real.

Sincerely,
India

Part V

Closing the Circle

Because transitions don't last forever, there'll come a time when you exit the cycle of a transition. Imagine a transition like a wheel divided into four quadrants, and as you travel clockwise, you start in the first quadrant by "entering the valley," then you shift down to the second lower right to a space of "settling in." Here you swing back and forth between "settling in" and "surrendering" both in the lower half. Eventually, you start moving toward completing the circle in the "direction" phase at the top left of the wheel. At this point, it becomes clear it will soon be time to close the circle, but that's not always so easy to do.

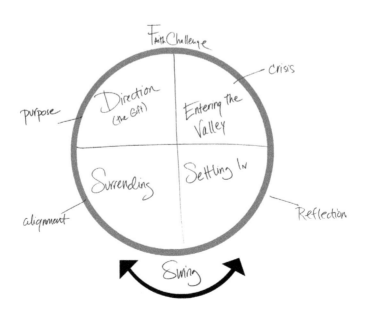

* Diagram adapted from the "Transitions Life Cycle" model detailed in the book, *Stuck! Navigating Life and Leadership Transitions* by Terry Walling. Used by permission.

I remember telling my coach that I knew my direction but I didn't know how to accomplish my purpose. He said, "Just wait for it. It will show up if it's God's will." He was referring to "destiny moments," which are occasions that show up to help facilitate the purpose. I was a bit skeptical, but it was amazing the many times God dropped opportunities in my lap that allowed me to fulfill the purpose that He had placed on my heart. God was directing my path, and I chose to be guided.

After I declared my purpose, I was put to the test. I remember vividly sitting in church and hearing the call. The director of our women's retreat stood up to make the announcement for the upcoming retreat. As I sat in the congregation, I heard God say "It's your turn." Four years prior, while at the retreat, I shared my aspiration to be a speaker with my best friend. So now God was pushing me to do just that. I reluctantly got up and made my way toward the director. I was being pushed; even my body language reflected my resistance to the call. Like a robot, I was taking jerky steps forward, not fully committed to this new idea that popped up in my head only a few minutes earlier. *Maybe I should wait and think on it a little more*, I thought. I was having a battle between two inner voices, one demanding I backpedal and the other pushing me closer to the director. I finally made it. There I stood in front of her, and I heard myself volunteer to lead a workshop. This was God at work, and I'm so grateful I listened, even though it took all my being to follow through with the call. I'm happy to report the workshop went off without a hitch and I accomplished a goal I had voiced years earlier.

These faith challenges will do exactly that—*test your faith*. According to Terry Walling, "it's a time when you go out on a limb, and you hear the chainsaw behind you." And don't be surprised if you have more than one faith challenge.

To me, this book has been the ultimate faith challenge. To put myself out there and let everyone know my weaknesses and vulnerabilities was scary, but my purpose is so much larger than my fear. This overwhelming need to help others has been placed on my heart for a reason, and I like to think it's because it's aligned with God's will.

When the day comes and you are closing the circle of a transition, I hope that you can look back and see the *reward* in the transition. As painful as it is and may have been, I guarantee there's something to gain from it.

Life After Divorce

To find a rainbow, you must weather the storm.
—Unknown

When I was still married, we moved our family to California from Georgia, and we bought a house to renovate. I had to pick paint colors for the walls, and I will never forget the name of one of the colors. Dunn-Edwards chose to call the blue that adorned my kitchen walls *Smoke and Mirrors*. Ironically, *smoke and mirrors* also accurately described my marriage in its final years. I still live in the house today, and when I see the extra can of paint in my garage, I cannot help but chuckle at the foreshadowing held in a paint's name.

From the outside, we looked like we were living the dream. Even my husband's wardrobe reflected the look of leisure. White linen pants, Gucci flip-flops, custom-made dress shirts, and a designer fedora were staples in his closet. He gave the air of living on *permanent vacation*. We had the beautiful large house overlooking the Pacific Ocean and two little girls attending the local elementary school. He took trips halfway around the world just to surf. Luxury cars lined our driveway. We were living large, and it showed in our lifestyle from our clothes to the extravagant vacations on private jets. Money was abundant in our lives, and my husband was skilled at making it. People looked at us and thought, *They have it all.*

I'm here to tell you it was all camouflage, but I didn't recognize the smoke screen we had created until my marriage came crashing down. In reality, my husband worked like a maniac. Work became *home*, and *home* became work. When he was physically present in the house, he was emotionally vacant, often distracted by some sort of Apple device. We took separate vacations. His halfway-around-the-world surf trip was one of them. He ran from his family. I was lonely, and I didn't have a partner in the marriage. We shared nothing. There was a massive gaping hole between us. It was the space where God was supposed to reside. Instead, money, distractions, and possessions were stuffed in the cavernous hole in attempt to quell any feelings of unhappiness and restlessness. "How much is enough?" was a recurring question I continued to ask him, but there was no cap, no magic number, because no amount would ever be enough.

Let me just say, I don't have a problem with success and making money or fabulous vacations for that matter, but I do have an issue when the love of money becomes the idol in the household. There I was living a life of polarity—one foot planted in the shallow ground of materialism with my husband and the other foot rooted in a sacred space of spiritual growth. I was taking the kids to church and hosting Bible studies at my house as I watched my husband throw lavish events promoting materialism and debauchery. I was living a life of incongruence and contradiction.

I observed my husband dissatisfied, unfulfilled, and restless. I convinced him to attend church, hoping he would connect with something—a person, a sermon, anything. Judging by his panic-stricken face, bugged-out eyes, and sweaty palms, my idea had gone awry.

As I drew closer to God, my husband drew farther away from me. We were moving in opposite directions, and money couldn't rescue us. Our marriage was broken, missing God, the very thing that could have saved us. I was still holding on to the idea of marriage, even though looking back now, it didn't resemble any kind of partnership. The marriage was off-kilter, teetering on the edge, displaying its extravagant imbalance, but I was blind to it.

You may be asking me, *how could you not see the divorce coming?* My answer is fear. Fear recoils from uncertainty. Even though I wasn't comfortable with my husband's flashy display of wealth, I enjoyed the lifestyle. I didn't enjoy feeling lonely and unloved, but life was not complicated. To be honest, I didn't see the brokenness in my marriage until years after the divorce.

It's common for most people to coast through a mediocre life because they don't want to face an outcome of uncertainty. God intended for us to live a rewarding and fulfilling life, not a mediocre existence. That's why when you can't do it yourself, God will do it for you.

Divorce hit me square between the eyes, chaos followed, and eventually I could see our brokenness. Now almost five years after my divorce, I can honestly say I had no idea life could be so amazing. I always believed in love. Even though I had been hurt so deeply, I still believed in marriage too. I knew I could have it. Along the way, I made a point to always write out what my ideal life would look like. There's power in the written word, and I often scribbled down a description of the man I wanted as my future husband. After many flawed relationships, I would go back to the drawing board and bring my list of the ideal man up-to-date. Don't get me wrong; I'm not insinuating life is not worth living without a man. I know many women that are perfectly content being single. But I know myself, and I liked being a wife. I liked the role, and I'm good at it.

As I was saying, my list looked something like this: "godly, family man, honest, loving, athletic, passionate, nice hands, likes to dance, can cook, loves being home, doesn't define himself by money, generous, gregarious, likes to travel, handy, tall, tall"—you get the idea. The list goes on for a while, but notice, I wrote *tall* twice. And tall is what I got! A six foot five former USA pro rugby player with the nickname *Chief* walked into my life two and half years after my divorce, but there was a huge problem. He was not of faith. He was spiritual, meaning he believed in God, but Jesus never made the cut.

He was into *new age* spirituality. In fact, he had followed James Ray, a motivational speaker who ended up serving time for the deaths of three of his attendees at a sweat lodge in Sedona. Chief was in the sweat lodge the day that tragedy happened. Thank goodness, God had a plan, and Chief made it out. Not only is it a mind-blowing story; it proves I had a seeker on my hands. He just happened to be seeking the wrong guy. I didn't push, and I listened, harboring unease about his lack of faith. It was something that constantly nagged me.

As time passed and we became more serious, the faith talk was unavoidable. I basically told him, "If we want to take this relationship any further, we need to be aligned in the spiritual department, or it won't work." Speaking from experience with my ex-husband, I knew the relationship would inevitably break down if we were not united in faith, a fundamental cornerstone of marriage.

This man listened to me, and he dived headfirst into Bible studies, church, and prayer meetings to learn and explore a religion he knew very little about. He and I both knew he couldn't do it for me. It was an undertaking he had to tackle all on his own. And if my faith didn't resonate with him, sadly, the relationship would have come to an abrupt end. I'm happy to say he embraced God with open arms and we are engaged to be married.

The transformation that has happened in front of my eyes is so much larger than anything I could have ever asked for. I prayed for a Christian man, and I got one, but God gave me something so much larger than that. He made a good man into a godly man, and I'm honored to soon call him my husband. Again and again, God continues to remind me He knows best, and my prayers are never as big and bold as what He has in store for me.

Before I arrived to this space, I had to learn. The road was harsh and full of pain, but what an incredible education I received in the valley of divorce. I made many mistakes along the way, but those mistakes were never failures. Those mistakes brought me closer to the life and the love I was meant to have. God wanted this for me all along. Finally, I have arrived, and it feels good. I am beyond grateful for this life, and my advice to you is always be aware of the gentle whisper of God saying "This is all my doing."

Chief and India, May 6, 2017

Blooper Reel

Humor has the ability to rise above any situation,
even if only for a few seconds.

—Viktor Frankl

Laughter is definitely one of my coping skills, but I say, it's better than having a drinking problem! I hope you are taking note of the humor in your life and creating a mental blooper reel that you get to share with others one day. I remember my oldest daughter at six years old asked me, "Is this all one big movie?" (meaning "Is this life one long movie?") My answer was yes. "It is in fact, so you better make it count!"

I'm telling you, dear reader, make your movie count, but hang on to the blooper reel. Life is funny, and from my experience, reality is much more entertaining than fiction. I don't know about you, but I certainly noticed the day I started laughing again. The early days of divorce were somber and heavy. When the laughter came back, I took note. It was evidence of my healing and the progress I made. I cringe at some of the things I did in the beginning, but at least now I can laugh at myself.

One day in particular, I was at the gym, and it was early in the separation. My yoga instructor asked me, "How's your man doing? Did he ever try yoga?" I heard myself say "My man left." It was straight out of a country song, as if Loretta Lynn said it herself. It was a shocking statement, and no sooner had I said it than I deflated into the arms of this man, crying in the middle of the gym. I look back at this now, I laugh, and I believe I could have written a decent country song in the midst of such misery.

Not only will you make gaffes, but so will the people around you in reaction to your divorce. And advice is one topic that seems to bring out the awkwardness in people. Most of the time, they are just trying to help, but they give you lousy advice when you're still mourning. Try not to hold it against them. They don't know what to say, and they will give you boneheaded opinions.

Just a few weeks after the breakup, when the dust had not even settled from my husband's marital demolition, a close family member offered her opinion on why my husband had left. She said, "When you're done, you're done." *Ouch!* I don't know how she thought that would help me, but I know she could have used a big dose of mindfulness and a shot of tact.

Another favorite line was "Now you should get a boob job." I guess this was an attempt to stick it to my ex-husband. I'm so thankful I didn't take her advice and seek vengeance through my breasts.

People will place themselves in your shoes to feel what you feel. That's what we do as humans, and it's a sign of compassion. But sometimes, I sensed that the other person speaking to me was scared my divorce was somehow contagious. They feared this could happen to them too. Then they avoided me. You may lose friends, but view it as trimming the fat in your circle. Divorce is the ultimate character detector. Friends with your same values will stick around.

Relatives will act strange too. After the divorce, I received a returned gift from a close family member. My ex-husband and I had given her a Christmas ornament years earlier when we were still married. It still boggles my mind why she felt compelled to send the gift back to me—maybe so I could hang it on my tree every year and be reminded of how the marriage didn't work and how this ornament no longer held any meaning. Instead, every year I hang it on the tree, and I laugh at what blatant awkwardness this ornament caused her. The point is, people will exhibit bizarre behavior during this time in your life. Don't hold it against them. We are all human, and we all have graceless days.

Like my daughter imagined, this life is one big movie, so make it count! Don't focus on the low points. We all have them. Look at all the joy around you. Allow the bloopers of life to amuse you, and be sure to take note of the small advances you make. They may seem insignificant at the time, but they end up representing major progress. Laughter in itself is *huge* progress. Humor is what we do to survive, so hang on to that blooper reel. Write it down and record your embarrassing moments. Your blunders will help someone else one day, and they will show you just how far you have come.

There will also be actions you take that may look insignificant on the surface, but in fact, they are quite symbolic, representing the leaps and bounds of progress you have made. When I was married, I gave my husband a bottle of Chanel cologne that I loved. It was called Egoïste, which means "selfish" and "self-seeking." Hmm, maybe I should have thought that one through before giving this bottle of "narcissism" to my husband. He never was a huge fan of it, but he wore it sometimes for my benefit.

When we separated, he left the cologne behind. So there it sat on the counter, a reminder that he was gone. I moved the cologne with me from house to house. It always sat in the same spot on the counter, next to my blue glass-bottled perfume. Occasionally, I would spray it and take in its fragrance. Then one day, I looked at that bottle for the last time. I took the cap off, and I smelled it. I asked myself, *Why do you have this? It holds nothing for you.* I didn't even like the scent anymore. The cleaners were in the kitchen finishing up. I rushed downstairs and gave the full bottle of "narcissism" to a father and his son. They probably always wondered why that bottle took up space on my bathroom counter. There was no man in the house, and judging by its contents, no one was using it. I'm not one to hold on to things I don't use, but this relic stayed with me for a while. Once I did let go of it, I realized I was letting go of so much more than a bottle of cologne.

We hold on to relics of our past because we are not ready to let go. Another leftover of my marriage was a six-foot photograph that hung on my wall. It was a picture of Byron Bay, a famous surf spot in Australia. A friend asked me what my connection was to Byron Bay. I choked back the tears as I explained I had no attachment and, in fact, it was quite the opposite; I had an aversion to the place. It was the spot where my ex-husband vacationed without me. My friend wasn't expecting my tearful reaction, but neither was I. I was shocked the photograph stirred such emotion in me. It made me realize I had a piece of art hanging in my home, my space, my sanctuary that caused me pain. His casual question inspired a new attitude in me. From that point forward, I made a pact with myself: if I didn't like something and I had the power to change it, well then, it was my duty to *change it*.

I painted over the photograph. I didn't even bother removing it from its frame. I applied paint to glass. Now I admire a beautiful ocean scene and snicker at the layer that sits beneath it—a layer of pain. What had brought me sadness now brings me joy. That painting is a lot like you and me. After we process a transition, we have a new exterior, but there in us lie many layers that contribute to the beautiful souls that we have become.

Dear beautiful soul, I hope this book has brought you encouragement, wisdom, and guidance through the valley of divorce. This book has been me *calling back* to you, giving you direction and hope. Now, I pass the baton to you. When you're ready, do as I did, and call back to those who walk your same path. Go share your story with others. Be an inspiration. Be the *hollaback* girl! But mostly, be thankful for this journey and this life.

"Layers of the Soul" 2013

Postscript

What If?

And now, Lord, with your help,
I shall become myself.
—Soren Kierkegaard

I have been pondering the question, What if I had known what I do now back in my twenties, would I still have married my first husband? The answer is, without a doubt, *yes*. First, I have two amazing daughters that would not have come into existence without the matrimony. Also, my ex-husband made me laugh for fifteen years, and I am forever grateful. We will always be spiritually connected, just like that first day I saw him in fifth grade in the bright-red parachute pants and I intuitively knew this person was a part of me. In addition, the wisdom I have gained on this journey is so much bigger than the short-lived pain I endured during the divorce.

I look at my precious life, and I know now that it couldn't have played out any other way. Call it what you want, but I call it destiny directed by God. I'm certain there are many reasons for our union besides our daughters, but only God is privy to that information. In the end, there was no way we, as partners, would have stayed aligned. It was evident that the trajectory of our lives was to veer, and he happened to be the first one to deviate. Now as I look back, I clearly see my line of direction was moving closer to God while my ex-husband's was receding, never aimed in His direction.

This realization inspires me to no longer take the actions of my ex-husband as a direct assault on my heart. It happened as it did because it was supposed to. And when I look at the long chapters of my marriage and divorce, I'm positive this was part of my human experience, leaving me with the choice of expansion or regression.

I chose expansion. I found purpose through pain, healing through self-exploration, and strength through a deepened relationship with Christ. I cannot fathom how anyone survives divorce without God in the picture. You can power through this valley alone, maybe never fully recovering from divorce, or you can walk, leaning on a Father who will give you strength to heal completely. With God as my shepherd, I became myself on the walk through the valley. I pray and hope that you too will become *yourself* along the walk through the valley of divorce. God bless you.

On the Fringe of the Valley

*And the wild things roared their terrible roars and
gnashed their terrible teeth and rolled their terrible
eyes and showed their terrible claws.*
—Maurice Sendak,
Where the Wild Things Are

I write how to triumphantly defeat fear, but I still deal with it, especially when I'm pulled back into court and I find myself *on the fringe of the valley*; it makes practicing what I preach to be a real challenge.

Even though I know I have a strong case, I despise fighting it out in court. If you had a supersmooth divorce, kudos to you for not giving all the money to the lawyers. But if you struggle with uninvited legal battles, listen up. There's a chance that your ex-spouse has a high-conflict personality. Most of the time, the ongoing fight in court has very little to do with money or child custody, but instead, it's more about control, connection, and the petitioner's distortion of reality. Many times, the high-conflict person is dealing with their own internal emotional crises and then projects it onto the safest person to hate, which may be you. High-conflict people want to stay connected, even if it means having an adversarial relationship. So if you find yourself in a ceaseless legal battle that you have not instigated, you may be dealing with a high-conflict personality.

Not only are the high-conflict personalities clogging up our legal system; the discord between parents is damaging the children involved. The children are plugging into the turbulent space between their parents and taking on the stress. With that being said, if you're the one that continues to drag your ex back to court, take a self-assessment. Question the motives behind your need for the fight. Is it worth the harm you are doing to your kids? I myself had to take a good, hard look at what I was risking by avoiding court and its uncomfortableness. I realized the legal battle was unfortunate but necessary. It was extremely necessary because I needed to stand up for myself.

Writing this book has been a deep dive into the study of India. Recently, I documented all the people, places, and things that impacted my life, and I came up with three acts that summed up my timeline. I named act 1 "Spectacular Dysfunction," act 2 "The Storm," and act 3 "This Beautiful Life." By doing this, I discovered a common theme woven throughout my life's chapters and throughout this book. You should already know it by now, but the common thread was my remarkable ability to ignore dysfunction. I came into this world being taught how to look past it, and I also had a knack for attracting it. I built a home and a family on a shoddy foundation. I saw the warning signs, but I wasn't aware enough to question the issues at hand. I don't blame myself, nor do I blame my family. Instead, I see it as the way I was supposed to learn my lesson.

After the storm of divorce blew through my life, I had to face my role as the enabler who allowed unacceptable behavior. I facilitated dysfunctional relationships even after my divorce because I allowed high-conflict behavior to be a part of my life. I didn't know any better.

But now, I don't have to accept it *ever* again. It's time for me to break every chain linking me to toxic high-conflict relationships, and I had a lot of them.

As a teen, I was a basketball player who daydreamed my way through practices and games. I really ticked off my coaches, one in particular named Coach B. He used to yell millimeters away from my face, spitting and sputtering in exasperation to my blatant indifference to follow his instructions. He had no idea I already had a lot of experience ignoring the roar of my father's booming voice every night. I would look at him as if I was listening, but in reality, I was thinking how very large his nose was and how it didn't exactly fit on his face. After ignoring the ranting, I would go back on the court and make the exact same mistake. Sometimes, I honestly thought his heart was going to stop right there on the basketball court. I envisioned the EMTs coming in to revive him after my antics, but these were not antics; they were simply my coping mechanism.

To be honest, he had no business screaming at me. I was just a kid. This would never happen today, but then again, we drank tab, played in creeks with water moccasins, and didn't use sunscreen or wear bike helmets. It was before we knew better.

Now, I know better, and I don't just cope. Today, I understand, and to understand is to know, and to know is to do better. I know there'll be times when you and I are pulled back in the valley, and this is when we are required to confront the big ugly monster of fear square in the face, with its unreasonably large nose, and know life is 100 percent guaranteed to bring troubles, and when the monster is spitting and sputtering his misery on you, you must just smile, knowing God's got you 100 percent. God gave us spiritual gifts, and fear was not one of them!

* Discoveries detailing the correlation between high-conflict people and ongoing litigation disputes are based on the book *"High Conflict People in Legal Disputes"* by Bill Eddy.

About the Author

India L. Kern is a divorce recovery mentor, an artist, a mother of two daughters, and a wife to Chief, her husband, Bill Leversee. She is also a yoga instructor and owner of Faithful Warrior Christian Yoga. India writes about transitions or the valleys of life where the soil is rich for wisdom, insight, and awareness. India teaches others how to discover the gift that God places in the valleys of hardship. She believes all transitions can lead to the discovery of a purpose-driven life.

India views divorce as a universal epidemic that needs to be addressed. That's what drove her to study life coaching and become a mentor of divorce recovery and self-development.

CPSIA information can be obtained
at www.ICGtesting.com
Printed in the USA
FSHW011549221218
54415FS